Avenues

Teacher's Resource Book

HAMPTON-BROWN

Contents

Masters to Support Language and Literacy Development

Writing Project Masters

Student Writing Samples

Family Newsletters
in English, Spanish, Vietnamese, Chinese, Korean, Hmong, and Haitian Creole

Inherited Traits

Study the pictures.
Look in a mirror or at your hand to see which traits you have.
Make a mark in each column that names a trait you have.
Make marks for traits your parents have.

Trait		Me	Mom	Dad
1.	attached earlobes			
2.	free earlobes			
3.	curled tongue			
4.	dimples			
5.	bent pinkies			
6.	straight pinkies			

What traits did you inherit from your parents? How do you know?

_____

Bookmark

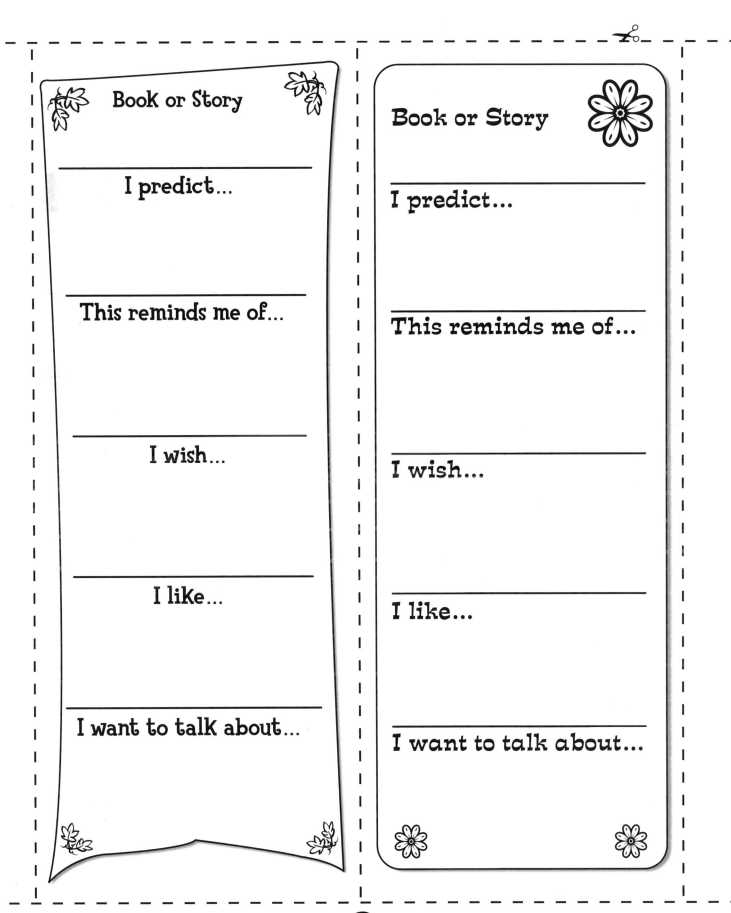

Book or Story

_____
I predict...

_____
This reminds me of...

_____
I wish...

_____
I like...

_____
I want to talk about...

Book or Story

_____
I predict...

_____
This reminds me of...

_____
I wish...

_____
I like...

_____
I want to talk about...

A Letter from Grandma

Dear Grandson,

    I'm glad you're coming to visit me again this summer. I have some new **records** for us to play. Best of all, Sammy sent me his new **album**. It was recorded live at the concert we went to! It **captures** the excitement of that special night. We can **play** it over and over.

    Did you know that Rafael Cortijo and his **band** are going to give another concert here? Of course, we will go! Sammy will get us seats in the front row. We can dance on the stage, so remember to **pack** your dancing shoes!

                 Love,
                  Grandma

We Honor Our Ancestors

Carl Angel's parents told him stories about dreams and adventures.

Hung Liu's grandmother made beautiful shoes from scraps of old cloth.

JoeSam.'s aunts wore colorful clothes. They brought the warmth of Africa and the West Indies to cold New York winters.

Patssi Valdez's mother worked hard for her family.

Fluency: Phrasing

Listen to the pauses the reader makes.
Mark short pauses with one line (/).
Mark longer pauses with two lines (//).

My Mother and Father
Trinidad Angel and Carlos Angel
by Carl Angel

My parents' stories are like hot cocoa on a cold night. They warm me up and comfort me. Mom tells me stories about her dreams. I remember her story of Bangus, the milkfish. If he swims into your dreams, it means good fortune the next day.

Dad tells me stories of real-life adventure. I'd imagine him as a boy during World War II dodging enemy bombs in the Philippines, or later on, as a sailor in the U.S. Navy, traveling to strange new places.

That's Dad in the Sun and Mom in the Moon, and me in between, riding the milkfish. The words are from my Mom's stories.

A Journal Entry About Ancestors

The people in "We Honor Our Ancestors" are a lot like people in my family. My mother tells stories to **comfort** me. My grandfather tells stories of **courage** and **adventure**. My uncle tells funny stories. I can always **trust** him to make me feel good. Just his **presence** makes me happy.

Storytelling is part of my **heritage**. I want to carry on the tradition. My family will be **proud** of me!

Ring of Fire Map

Draw at least 5 volcanoes on the map. Each volcano should be in a different country. Label each volcano. Write a caption that tells about the Ring of Fire.

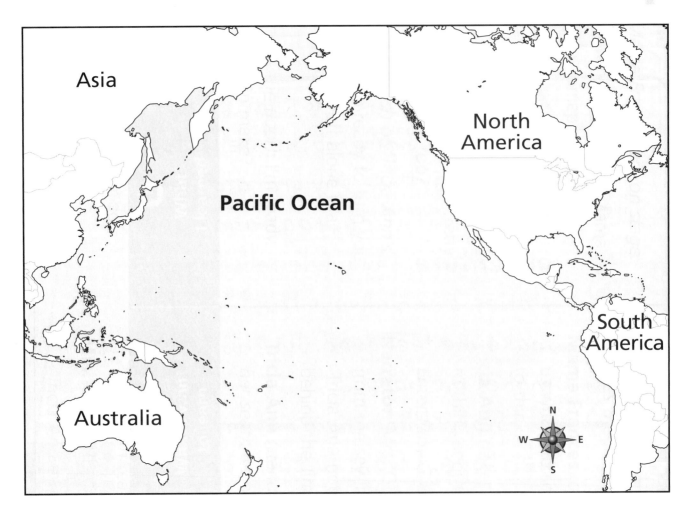

What is the "Ring of Fire?" How did it get its name?

_____

_____

_____

Name _____ Date _____

Reflection Journal

Page	My question	The answer

A Letter from Mei Yoon

Dear Grandmother,

Thank you for telling me a **superior** story. Toh was so **clever**! I got the point of the story, too. Now, I enjoy my **stitching**. It's not a **task** anymore. Plus, when I'm finished, I'm proud of my **handiwork**.

In fact, I have decided to enter a quilting **contest**. I want to show the **beauty** of the earth and sky on my quilt. Do you have any small pieces of **material** that I can use for it?

I hope you will tell another story soon!

Love,

Mei Yoon

The Woman Who Fell from the Sky

An Iroquois Tale

Long ago, there was no land, just the sky above and the water below. One day, the huge tree that grew in the center of Sky-World fell over and ripped a hole through the clouds. Sky Woman leaned over to see what was below the clouds, and she fell through the hole! She tried to grab the tree's branches to stop herself, but she got only a handful of seeds.

The water animals wanted to stop her fall. Muskrat came up from the bottom of the water with a bit of mud in his paws. He placed the mud on Turtle's back and it spread out to become the whole world. That is why some tribes call Earth "Turtle Island."

When Sky Woman came safely to Earth, she dropped the seeds from the Sky Tree on the new soil. The first plants grew from these seeds.

Maui Fishes the Hawaiian Islands
A Hawaiian Legend

Long ago, there lived a trickster named Maui. Maui's brothers said he wasn't a good fisherman. To prove them wrong, Maui got a special hook and set out to catch a giant fish.

Something bit on the hook! Maui pulled with all his strength to haul the fish in. Finally, something came out of the ocean. Maui saw that he had pulled the Hawaiian Islands out of the sea!

Maui thought the Sun should stay over his islands longer so people would have more time to fish. He made a net and caught the Sun. In return for freedom, the Sun agreed to make the days longer in summer and shorter in winter.

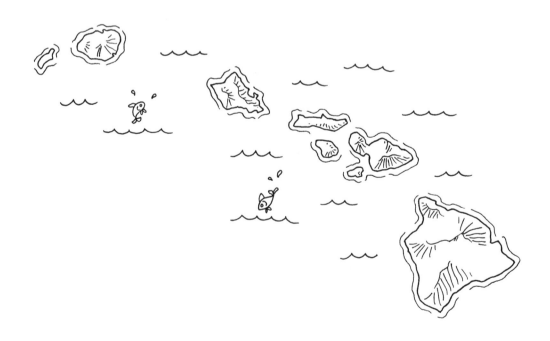

Research an Animal

Use this chart to take notes about your animal.

Animal and Scientific Name	Description	Habitat and How It Adapts to Its Environment	Dangers to Its Survival

More notes:

Planet Earth/Inside Out

1. Earth is formed.	Space dust and gases mixed together to make the Earth. Long ago, oceans covered the land. Then the land split into continents.
2. Earth has layers.	Earth's center is a solid ball of metal. Around Earth's center is melted metal. Above that is partly melted rock. Earth's thin crust is on top.
3. The plates of Earth's crust move.	Plates are pieces of the Earth's crust. Plates move slowly. Plates slide, move apart, and bump together.
4. Earthquakes happen.	Faults are cracks in the Earth's crust. Plates push against each other and cause earthquakes.
5. Volcanoes erupt.	Pressure below the surface makes a hole in the Earth's crust. Melted rock called magma explodes out of the hole.
6. Earth is always changing.	Plates push up to make mountains. Plates move apart to make valleys. Huge ice sheets, glaciers, shape the Earth. People change the Earth, too.

A Letter to Gail Gibbons

Dear Ms. Gibbons,

Your book about the Earth is awesome! Now I understand what happens when a **volcano** erupts. I also learned that **gravity** pulled the Earth together.

I like to teach my brother things. Now I can tell him that Earth's **core** is hot metal. I can also explain the difference between the **mantle** and **crust**.

My mother says I never stand still. It's not me! It's because Earth's **plates** are always moving.

There was an **earthquake** in my state, but I didn't feel it. Was I too far away from the **fault**?

Sincerely,

Lee

Make a Seismograph

Materials: One-quart jar with lid, wax paper, felt-tip pen, rubber band, masking tape, scissors

rubber band   felt-tip pen
tape
wax paper

1. Fill your jar with water and put the lid on it.

2. Cut a long strip of wax paper and place it on a table.

3. Set the jar of water on one end of the wax paper.

4. Use a rubber band to attach the pen, point down, to the jar.

5. Position the pen so the felt tip touches the paper. Tape the pen to the jar, and set it near one end of the paper.

6. Then, during the "earthquake," steadily pull the paper straight out from under the jar.

Richter Scale

An earthquake's size depends upon how much energy it releases. Another word for *size* is *magnitude*. Earthquakes are measured in magnitudes.

Magnitudes	Earthquake Effects
M1 to M3:	Generally not felt, but recorded
M3 to M4:	Often felt, but causes no damage
M5:	Felt widely, slight damage near epicenter
M6:	Causes slight to major damage to buildings
M7:	Major earthquake; can cause serious damage
M8:	Great earthquake; can cause great damage

Recycling Facts

Sources for Different Products

Product	Made from
plastic	oil
glass	sand
paper, cardboard	trees
cans	aluminum
tires	rubber trees or oil and coal

Recycling Facts

1. Recycling one ton of paper saves: 17 trees, 6,953 gallons of water, 463 gallons of oil, 587 pounds of air pollution, and enough energy to power a TV for 31 hours.

2. It takes 500,000 trees to make the amount of newsprint that Americans throw away each week.

3. The energy saved from recycling one glass bottle is enough to run a TV for 3 hours or a 100-watt light bulb for 4 hours.

4. Glass never wears out. It can be recycled again and again.

5. Recycling one ton of glass saves the same amount of energy we get from ten gallons of oil.

6. Non-food containers, carpet, plastic rulers, and clothing can all be made from recycled plastic.

7. Turning off the water faucet when brushing your teeth can save 9 gallons of water every time you brush.

Unit 2 | Earth: The Inside Story
© Hampton-Brown

19

Master 16
For use with TE pp. T115a–T115b

Exercise Schedule

To be healthy, you need at least one hour of exercise every day.
Make a schedule that shows how you will get enough exercise this week.

My Exercise Schedule

Day	Activity	Time
Monday		
Tuesday		
Wednesday		
Thursday		
Friday		
Saturday		
Sunday		

Dancing Wheels

1 The dancers get ready. They put on makeup. They put on costumes. Some dancers walk onto the stage. Other dancers wheel onto the stage. The Dancing Wheels show begins.

2 Mary Verdi-Fletcher dances from her wheelchair. Mary's parents taught her to think of what she could do. Mary learned to dance. Then she started the dance company Dancing Wheels.

3 Devin and Jenny dance together. They practice a lot. Devin loves to dance, but he doesn't tell his friends. They might make fun of him.

4 The dancers practice all day. They perform in the show. Mary is happy that she didn't listen to other people. She is glad she learned to dance.

Fluency: Phrasing

Listen to the pauses the reader makes.
Mark short pauses with one line (/).
Mark longer pauses with two lines (//).

Dancing Wheels

Mary watches the young dancers rush offstage. Devin and Jenny hurry to change their costumes. They have lead roles in the main dance on today's program. Jenny almost barrels into three people, calling out "Sorry! Sorry!" as she whips by. Devin complains again about wearing tights today. Little Sabatino hitches a ride on a sit-down dancer's chair.

Young Sabatino came to live in Cleveland when Mary invited his parents to work with her and the Dancing Wheels company. She thought they were the right people to keep her crazy idea going. So the Verlezzas came.

A Letter from Jenny

Dear Devin,

I can't believe the fall **performance** is over! We worked so hard to get every **movement** right (except when we were goofing around). I thought I was out of **energy** after so much practice. Now I want to rehearse for the spring show!

I know the **audience** loved our dance. You danced with so much **expression**. Of course, your wonderful partner helped you **improve**. Isn't that right? I'm just kidding. You would be a great dancer with any partner. Don't get a new one, though!

Your friend,

Jenny

Evaluation Form

1 Who gave the review?

_____

2 What performance did the speaker review?

_____

3 Who was the audience?

☐ my partner   ☐ teacher and class

4 What was the language like?

☐ formal   ☐ informal

5 What was the speaker's purpose?

☐ to give information   ☐ to entertain   ☐ to persuade

6 Was the presentation right for the purpose, audience, and occasion?

☐ yes   ☐ no

Budget Planner

Item	Cost
Theater rental	$_____
Performers: _____ performers x $_____ =	$_____
Director	$_____
Stage hands: _____ stage hands x $_____ =	$_____
Costumes: _____ costumes x $_____ =	$_____
Props	$_____
Other expenses: _____	$_____

TOTAL COSTS: $_____

To make a 10% profit, our total ticket sales need to be $ _____.
(**Hint:** Find the sum of your total costs plus 10% of your total costs.)

We need to sell _____ tickets.

(**Hint:** Divide your total ticket sales by the cost of one ticket.)

How Simple Machines Work

Machine	Example
Wheel and Axle A wheel and axle can carry a load across a distance. When axles connect two or more wheels, a load can rest on top of the axles. When the wheels spin, the wheels, axles, and load move forward.	When you put your dog in a wagon and pull it around the yard, you're using a wheel and axle.
Screw People use this simple machine to fasten things together. As it twists around, a screw drills through one object and then into the next. It holds the two objects tightly together.	You are using a screw when you fasten a bulb into a lamp. The spiral ridges on the tip of the bulb make it a screw.
Inclined Plane People push, roll, or slide things over an inclined plane instead of lifting them. The inclined plane makes it easier to move things from lower to higher places, or to slide things from higher to lower places.	A waterslide is an inclined plane. Kids slide down the inclined plane into a pool of water.

Unit 3 | Bodies in Motion
© Hampton-Brown

26

Master 23
For use with TE pp. T155a–T155b

How Simple Machines Work

Machine	Example
Lever When a person pushes down on one end of a lever, the other end can move a heavy object or pry something loose.	A seesaw is a lever used for fun. When a child on one side goes down, a child on the other side goes up!
Pulley When a person pulls down on the rope, the pulley lifts a heavy object from a low place to a higher place.	Did you ever watch someone pull down on a rope to make a flag go up the pole? They were using a pulley to raise the flag.
Wedge A wedge can help lift or tighten something. It can also help split something open. The thin edge is fitted into a slit or opening. Then the other end is hammered to drive the wedge in tighter.	An ax is a wedge. When the thin, sharp edge goes into a log, it makes an opening. Then the wider part of the ax follows and splits the wood apart.

Unit 3 | Bodies in Motion
© Hampton-Brown

27

Master 24
For use with TE pp. T155a–T155b

Amazing Facts

That's Amazing!

An amazing fact about _____

is _____

_____

I found it in the book _____

by _____

_____   _____
Name   Date

That's Amazing!

An amazing fact about _____

is _____

_____

I found it in the book _____

by _____

_____   _____
Name   Date

Fluency: Phrasing

Listen to the pauses the reader makes.
Mark short pauses with one line (/).
Mark longer pauses with two lines (//).

Moving

What happens to your body when you move? Your brain, nerves, muscles, and bones all work together to make you walk, run, or jump. You can also make smaller movements, such as a smile or a frown. You are always moving, even when you are asleep. Your heart and lungs move inside you to keep you alive.

There is a strong, hard framework of bones inside your body. This framework is called your skeleton. It holds your body up and keeps it from collapsing in a heap.

A Letter to Anita Ganeri

Dear Ms. Ganeri,

I really like your article. I liked learning about how my **muscles**, **nerves**, **bones**, and **heart** all work together to make me move. It's fun to see all the bones and **joints** of the **skeleton**. The **spinal cord** is fascinating, too.

I never knew how hard my body works. Even my tiny cells work to use **oxygen**! The next time my mother scolds me for sleeping too late, I can tell her I was working hard!

Your friend,

Kiana

Make a Diagram

Use this outline to draw a skeleton and internal organs.

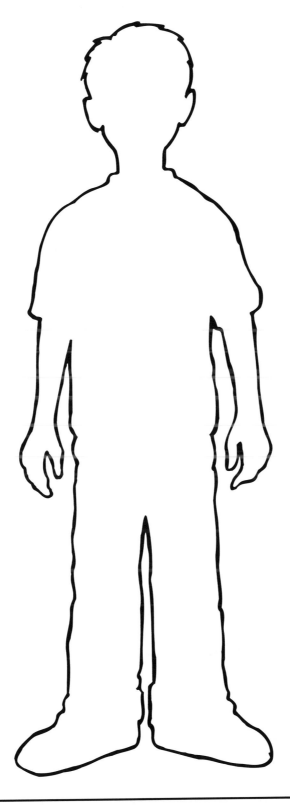

Life Expectancy in the United States

Use the information to make a graph.

Year	Life Expectancy in Years
1900	47
1910	50
1920	54
1930	60
1940	63
1950	68
1960	70
1970	71
1980	74
1990	75
2000	77

Unit 3 | Bodies in Motion
© Hampton-Brown

32

Master 29
For use with TE pp. T177a–T177b

Name _____   Date _____

The Value of Tea

Problem: In 1773, the American colonists protested a British tax on tea. They threw 324 chests of British tea into Boston Harbor. At the time, that tea was worth about 18,000 British pounds (£18,000). Today, British tea is worth 70 times what it was worth then. A British pound (£) today equals about $1.60 in U.S. money. How much would the tea be worth in the U.S. today?

1. Write the value of the tea in 1773 in pounds (£).   _____

2. Multiply line 1 times 70.   _____

3. Write what a pound (£) is worth in U.S. dollars ($) today.   _____

4. Multiply line 2 by line 3. Write a dollar sign ($).   _____

How do you think the British felt after the colonists dumped their tea? Why?

Joining the Boston Tea Party

Grandma and the twins go back in time to 1773. They go to Boston and meet Ben Reed. Ben tells them that the people of Boston are angry with King George of England. The king sent soldiers to Boston. He put a tax on everything people bought.

The colonists stop buying things from England. King George stops most taxes, but he keeps the tax on tea. The people meet. They decide to dump the English tea into the ocean.

The colonists go onto the ships. They open boxes of tea. They dump the tea in the water. Grandma says they helped start the American Revolution. Then Grandma and the twins go home.

Liz's Journal Entry

Grandma took us back in time again! This time we went to the Massachusetts **colony** in 1773.

The colonists were angry about King George's **politics**. They didn't even have a **representative** in the British Parliament. They didn't like the British **taxes**. They didn't like having British **soldiers** in the streets. They certainly didn't like being called **traitors**!

We helped the **patriots** dump tea into the harbor. Grandma said we helped start the revolution!

Theme Theater

The Old South Meeting House

Setting

On a Boston street and at the Old South Meeting House. The year is 1773.

Cast of Characters

Narrator 1   Narrator 2
Woman 1   Woman 2
Boy twin from the future   Ben
Girl twin from the future   Sam Adams
Governor Hutchinson   Colonists
Man 1   Man 2

Hutchinson (*pounding the gavel*)**:** I won't do it!

Sam Adams steps up to the podium. The governor sits.

Girl: What's going to happen now?

Ben: See that man? That's Sam Adams. He's going to give the signal.

Sam Adams (*at the podium*)**:** This meeting can do nothing more to save the country!

Boy and Girl: What now?

Ben: We're about to have a really big tea party. This tea party will go down in history!

End of play.

Unit 4 | Freedom's Trail
© Hampton-Brown

36

Master 33
For use with TE pp. T215a–T215b

Scene 1: A Street in Boston, 1773

Narrator 1: The colonists are not happy. The British Parliament tried to raise money by taxing their colonies, and the colonists complained, LOUDLY!

Narrator 2: So King George the Third stopped all taxes except one: the tax on tea.

Boy (looks around): Hey, Ben. Why is everyone so angry around here?

Ben: The English aren't treating us right. That's why! Why should we pay taxes? We don't get to say how the money is spent.

Boy: But there's only one tax.

Woman 1: Right! It's a tax on tea! We all love tea.

Girl: Why don't you drink hot chocolate then? It comes from America!

Woman 2: That's a great idea! Let's do it! We can have chocolate parties instead of tea parties.

Ben: Hey, let's *have* a tea party!

A confused look passes over colonists' faces.

Scene 2: Old South Meeting House, That Same Night

Narrator 1: That night thousands of people gather at the Old South Meeting House. Many people are angry.

Narrator 2: The twins and their cousin Ben enter. Angry colonists fill the church. They are talking loudly to one another. Some shout.

Hutchinson (pounding the gavel for quiet): Thank you for coming to our meeting.

Man 1: Governor Hutchinson! About those ships in the Boston Harbor . . .

Hutchinson: Yes.

Man 1: Send them back to England!

Hutchinson: Sir! They are full of tea.

Man 1: We will not pay the tax on tea!

Man 2: We will not pay a tax on anything! *Colonists shout things such as "Send them back!" and "No taxation without representation!"*

Unit 4 | Freedom's Trail
© Hampton-Brown

37

Master 34
For use with TE pp. T215a–T215b

Tea Party Messages

Say "No!" to King George's unfair taxes.

May I have a cup of tea, please?

Break open these boxes, and dump out the tea.

Meet us at the dock at seven tonight, and tell no one.

Come with me! Hide behind these boxes.

Go back to your homes. I will not let you on my ship!

1 What message is the person giving?

_____

2 Why am I listening?

☐ to be informed   ☐ to learn how to do something

☐ to be persuaded   ☐ to be entertained

3 What is the speaker's perspective, or what name would you use for the speaker?

☐ a loyalist   ☐ a patriot

4 What does the speaker want me to do?

_____

Word Detective

New Word: _____

What I think it means: _____

_____

Clues: _____

_____

Definition: _____

_____

_____
Name   Date

New Word: _____

What I think it means: _____

_____

Clues: _____

_____

Definition: _____

_____

_____
Name   Date

A Letter to George Washington

April 30, 1791

Dear Mr. President,

I am ten years old, and I live on the western **frontier**. I want to thank you for helping to build our **independent** country.

I am very proud of our **government**. I think that our **Constitution** is such an important document. Someday I hope to run for **Congress**.

I met a **delegate** to the Constitutional Convention. He **declares** that you are the best man to lead our country. I agree!

Respectfully,

Ira Danner

Facts About the United States

Size of the United States
Total Area: 9,629,091 square kilometers
about 0.5 times the size of South America
about 0.3 times the size of Africa
about 2.5 times the size of Western Europe

Features of the United States	
Coastline Length:	19,924 kilometers
Highest Point:	Mount McKinley: 6,194 meters
Lowest Point:	Death Valley: 86 meters

Population of the United States		
Ages	**Males**	**Females**
0–14 years	30,116,782	28,765,183
15–64 years	92,391,120	93,986,468
65 years and older	14,748,522	20,554,414

Name _____

Date _____

KWLQ Chart

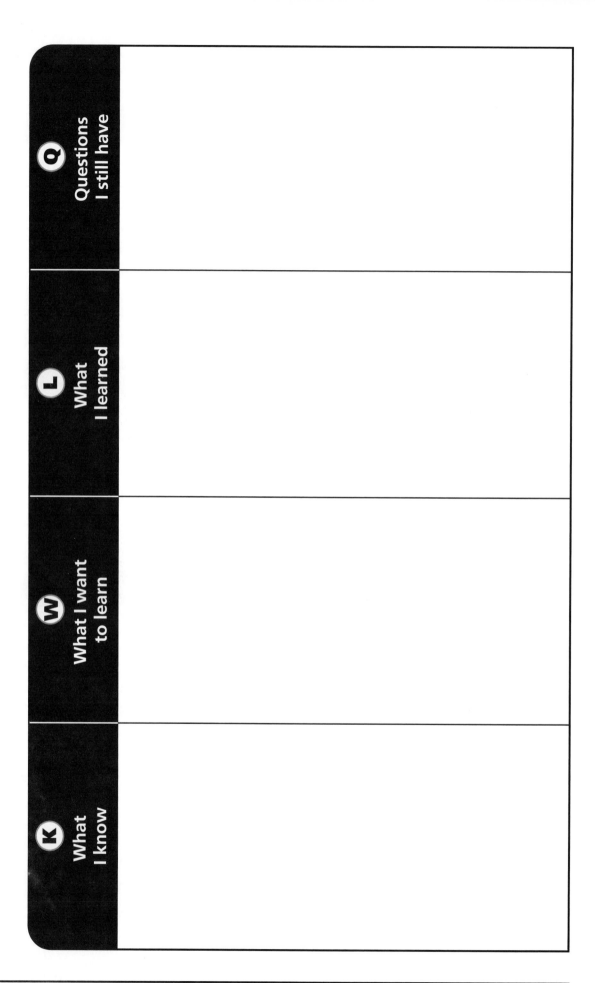

K What I know	**W** What I want to learn	**L** What I learned	**Q** Questions I still have

Fluency: Phrasing

Listen to the pauses the reader makes.
Mark short pauses with one line (/).
Mark longer pauses with two lines (//).

Greetings from America

In Wyoming, Montana, and Idaho,
Steaming geysers faithfully blow.

A blast of steam erupts through a hole in the Earth! Steaming hot water soars hundreds of feet into the air like a giant fountain. Then, just as suddenly, the eruption stops. The steam evaporates, and all is quiet for a while, until the steam erupts again! This natural exploding fountain is called a geyser.

More than half of all the geysers in the world are in Yellowstone National Park. About 200 of these are active geysers that may erupt. Yellowstone sits on a huge "hot spot" where hot melted rock, called magma, lies just a few miles below ground. The magma heats up underground water, and "whoosh!", a geyser blows its top.

A Letter from the West

Dear Grandpa,

This is the best vacation ever! The **landforms** in the West are amazing. First, we drove over the Rockies, a huge **mountain range**. I took a picture of Mom, Dad, and Ramiro by a **waterfall**. The next day, Mom took a picture of me at the bottom of a deep **canyon**.

Yesterday, we saw a **geyser** and then drove south along the **coastline**. Today Mom and Dad relaxed on the beach while Ramiro and I hiked through the **dunes** at Pismo Beach.

Wish you were here!

Love,

Rosa

Name _____ Date _____

Park Tour Evaluation Form

Delivery

Did the speaker smile and look happy?   ☐ Yes   ☐ No

Was the speaker energetic and excited?   ☐ Yes   ☐ No

How did that make you feel about the park?   ☐ Want to visit   ☐ Not interested

Audience

Who did the speaker seem to be talking to?   ☐ Kids   ☐ Adults

Did the speaker name things a kid likes?   ☐ Yes   ☐ No

How did that make you feel about the park?   ☐ Want to visit   ☐ Not interested

Language Choice

Did the speaker use words that made you
want to visit the park?   ☐ Yes   ☐ No

Did the speaker tell why he or she likes
the park?   ☐ Yes   ☐ No

How did that make you feel about the park?   ☐ Want to visit   ☐ Not interested

Describe how you felt after listening to the speaker.

_____

_____

Would you want to go to this park? Why or why not?

_____

_____

_____

Compare Oral Traditions

Northeastern Sailing Song: "Boston Come All-Ye!"

Come all ye young sailor men, listen to me,
I'll sing you a song of the fish of the sea.

Then blow ye winds westerly, westerly blow,
We're bound to the south'ard, so steady
    she goes!

Oh, first came the whale, the biggest of all;
He climbed up aloft and let every sail fall.

Up jumped the halibut, lay flat on the deck,
He said, "Mister Captain, don't step on
    my neck!"

The porpoise came next with his little snout,
He grabbed the wheel, calling "Turn her
    about!"

Up jumped the tuna saying, "I am the King!
Pull on the line and let the bell ring."

Western Song: "Get Along Little Dogies"

As I was a-walkin' one mornin' for pleasure
I spied a young cowboy come ridin' along,
His hat was thrown back and his spurs were
    a-jinglin',
As he approached me a-singin' this song.

Whoopee ti yi yo, get along little dogies,
It's your misfortune and none of my own,
Whoopie ti yi yo, get along little dogies
For you know Wyoming will be your
    new home.

Unit 5 | From Sea to Shining Sea
© Hampton-Brown

46

Master 43
For use with TE pp. T283a–T283b

Compare Oral Traditions

Appalachian Song: "Hush, Little Baby"

Hush, little baby, don't say a word.
Papa's gonna buy you a mocking bird.
And if that mocking bird won't sing,
Papa's gonna buy you a diamond ring.

And if that diamond ring turns brass,
Papa's gonna buy you a looking glass.
And if that looking glass gets broke,
Papa's gonna buy you a billy goat.

And if that billy goat won't pull,
Papa's gonna buy you a cart and bull.
And if that cart and bull turn over,
Papa's gonna buy you a dog named Rover.

And if that dog named Rover won't bark,
Papa's gonna buy you a horse and cart.
And if that horse and cart fall down,
You'll still be the sweetest little baby in town.

Southern Song: "Oh, John the Rabbit"

Oh, John the Rabbit, Yes ma'am,
Got a mighty habit, Yes ma'am,
Jumping in my garden, Yes ma'am,
Cutting down my cabbage, Yes ma'am,
My sweet potatoes, Yes ma'am,
My fresh tomatoes, Yes ma'am,
And if I live, Yes ma'am,
To see next fall, Yes ma'am,
I ain't gonna have, Yes ma'am,
No cotton at all, Yes ma'am.

Unit 5 | From Sea to Shining Sea
© Hampton-Brown

47

Master 44
For use with TE pp. T283a–T283b

The Bunyans

Paul Bunyan is a huge, strong man. He marries a giant woman named Carrie. Later, they have a son named Little Jean and a daughter named Teeny.

Teeny gets syrup in her hair. Bears crawl in to eat it! Pa Bunyan makes Niagara Falls to wash the bears out. Little Jean carves Bryce Canyon. The sand from his shoes makes the Great Sand Dunes.

Then the children go to the Pacific Ocean. Teeny rides whales. Jean carves Big Sur. On the way home, the family builds the Rocky Mountains.

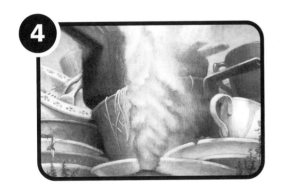

The Bunyans need to wash their huge dishes, so Ma digs a hole. Hot water, a geyser, shoots up. Then Jean and Teeny grow up and leave home. Ma and Pa Bunyan stop working and live happily.

Paul Bunyan Gets the Job Done

Winifred Winslow was in more trouble than a rabbit in a foxhole. She ran a logging camp, but all her lumberjacks had taken better jobs at another camp. It looked as though poor Winifred was going to go broke.

That's when Paul Bunyan showed up. Now Paul was no ordinary lumberjack. He was as strong and as fast as a herd of buffalo. He told Winifred he would do the work of fifty men for the wages, or pay, of five. Winifred happily agreed.

Paul got right to work. With his right arm, he chopped one hundred trees an hour. With his left arm, he trimmed the trees and stacked them neatly beside the sawmill. Babe, Paul's big blue ox, put the logs through the mill. Then Babe hauled the lumber to the market. As she dragged the heavy load, it dug a trench fifty feet wide. Paul flooded the trench and made it into a river. After that, they used the river to float the lumber to market.

At the end of the day, Babe was hungry and thirsty. Babe was the only family Paul had, so he always took very good care of her. He turned over a barn and filled it with hay for Babe to eat. Then he dug five enormous holes and filled them with water. Today Babe's drinking holes are called the Great Lakes.

When Winifred saw all that Paul and Babe had done, she knew her troubles were over. Paul ran her camp for years and became famous as the mightiest lumberjack in the United States.

Slue-Foot Sue

In the days when Texas was wilder than a coyote in a bad mood, there lived a gal named Slue-Foot Sue. Sue had the strength of ten men and could ride any critter on Earth. One day she spotted a catfish the size of a Texas longhorn. She put her fingers to her mouth, let out a whistle, and woke up folks clear to Mississippi. The catfish swam right to her, and Sue jumped on for a ride.

Sue was a-hootin' and a-hollerin' and having such a good time that she attracted the notice of the mighty cowboy Pecos Bill. There wasn't a hoss that Bill couldn't tame. He had once ridden a cyclone until it gave up and turned into a gentle breeze.

Bill fell in love with Sue as quick as a wink. His very first words to her were, "Howdy, purdy miss. Will you be my bride?" Sue agreed on one condition. She wanted to ride Bill's hoss Widowmaker. Bill begged Sue to ask for anything but that, but Sue would not change her mind. At last, Bill gave in.

Sue climbed up on Widowmaker and took off with a holler. Suddenly, the horse bucked and threw Sue clear into outer space. Sue bumped her head on the Moon and fell back to Earth. When she hit the ground, she bounced right up again. Sue bounced between the Earth and the Moon for days. Finally Bill roped her right out of the sky. Sue thanked Bill for saving her, and the two were hitched the very next day.

John Henry

On the night he was born, John Henry shook up the whole state of Virginia. He weighed forty-four pounds, and his first cry was so powerful that folks thought there had been an earthquake.

The boy began hammerin' things before he could crawl. By the time he was ten, he could pound in fence posts as fast as a grown man. His muscles were like steel.

When John Henry left home, he became a steel driver for the railroad company. The company was diggin' a tunnel through a solid rock mountain. John Henry's job was to pound a steel rod into the rock to make a hole for the dynamite. Most men could only swing a ten pound hammer for a few hours. John Henry could swing it all day.

One day, the job captain said he wanted to replace the steel drivers with a machine. John Henry was angry. He told the captain he could beat any machine. So the captain set up a contest between John and the steam-powered drill.

At first, the steam drill pounded away at the rock faster than John Henry, but soon John Henry picked up a second hammer and started swingin' with both arms. Soon he was winnin'. John worked for hours without stoppin'. In the end, John Henry was declared the winner. Yet the contest was too much, even for the strongest man in all of Virginia. After he won, the great steel driver laid down and died with his hammer still in his hand.

Fluency: Expression
Readers Theater Script

Storyteller: One day, Paul Bunyan discovered an enormous hole in the side of a hill. He climbed inside and saw a gigantic woman.

Paul: Hello there!

Carrie: Hello. I'm Carrie McIntie.

Storyteller: Paul saw Carrie's face, and it was love at first sight.

Paul: I'm Paul Bunyan. Why are you down here?

Carrie: I was sitting on the hill when my lucky wishbone fell into a crack in the earth.

Storyteller: Paul grinned as wide as the Missouri River. He reached into his shirt pocket. He pulled out a wishbone.

Paul: Look. I have one, too!

Carrie: I've been digging all day trying to find my wishbone.

Paul: Marry me, Carrie, and we'll share mine.

Storyteller: Carrie and Paul were married in the enormous cavern that Carrie had carved. It was so big that folks called it "Mammoth Cave."

A Letter from Teeny

Dear Little Jean,

   I just read in the newspaper that an **enormous** crowd waits every day to see your sculptures! Your **gargantuan** croquet player looks just like Ma. The **mammoth** lumberjack sculpture is great, too.

   I am coming to Venice soon. I'll take the **scenic** route. I want to see the **acres** of tulips in Holland first. Then I'll step over the **mighty** Alps.

   I had a **gigantic** fashion show last week. My hot-air-balloon skirts were a **huge** hit. I'll bring my favorite one. Maybe you'll even do a sculpture of me!

                                    Love,

                                    Teeny

Theme Theater Props

Unit 5 | From Sea to Shining Sea
© Hampton-Brown

54

Master 51
For use with TE pp. T305a–T305b

Theme Theater Props

Unit 5 | From Sea to Shining Sea
© Hampton-Brown

55

Master 52
For use with TE pp. T305–T305b

Make a 3-D Model

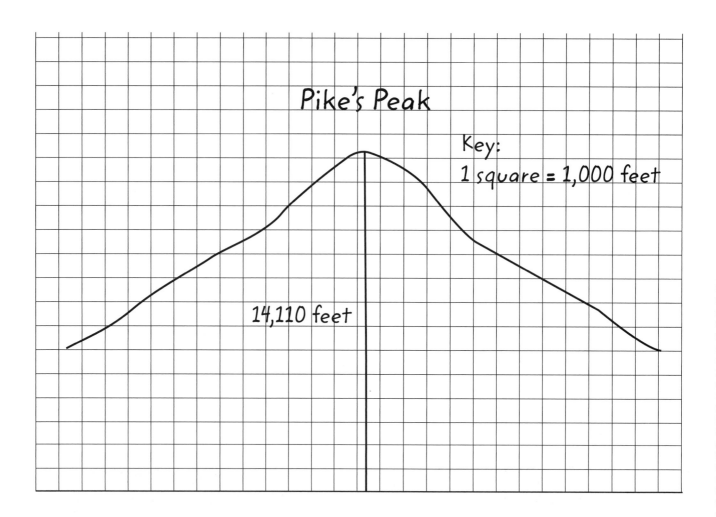

To make a scale model:

1. Decide how many feet or miles each square will represent. Make a key.

2. Make a scale drawing that matches your key.

3. Cut out the drawing.

4. Make a 3-D clay or papier mâché model the same size as your drawing. Also look at a photograph of the landform or waterway to make your model look realistic.

Lighting Costs

Read the fact box.
Complete the steps to calculate the cost of lighting your classroom for different periods of time. Then answer the question.

It costs 1¢ to light an incandescent bulb for 1 hour.

It costs 1¢ to light a fluorescent bulb for 4 hours, or ¼¢ for 1 hour.

1. Count the number of each kind of bulb in your classroom. Write the numbers in column 1.

2. Multiply the number of bulbs times the cost to run each for one hour. Write the answer in column 2.

3. Multiply the cost per hour times 6. Write the answer in column 3.

4. Multiply the cost per day times 5. Write the answer in column 4.

5. Multiply the cost per day times 20. Write the answer in column 5.

6. Multiply the cost per day times 185. Write the answer in column 6.

	Cost per Hour	Cost per Day	Cost per Week	Cost per Month	Cost per Year
Number of incandescent bulbs:					
Number of fluorescent bulbs:					

How should your school light its classrooms? Why?

_____

_____

Ben Franklin's Experiment

1 Katrina and her family visit a science museum. They see things Ben Franklin invented long ago. Then Katrina meets Ben Franklin! He tells her that he did not discover electricity, but he learned about it.

2 Katrina goes back in time with Ben. Ben proves that lightning is made of electricity. He uses this information to make houses safe from lightning.

3 Ben tells Katrina more about what he did and the things he invented. He tells Katrina that she can do a lot, too, but she must read and think carefully. Ben gives Katrina an old penny. It will remind her of what he taught her.

A Letter from Katrina

Dear Aunt Clare,

I had an amazing adventure this weekend! Mom, Dad, Carla, and I went to the Franklin Institute Science Museum. We all looked at an **exhibit** about Benjamin Franklin. What a great man! I can't believe one man could **accomplish** so much!

Some people think that he **invented** electricity, but they're wrong. I learned that he conducted an **experiment** to **prove** that **lightning** is a kind of electricity. How did I **discover** this? I met Ben Franklin in the museum!

Your niece,

Katrina

Inventions for Sale!

A very important invention!

SMITH

MINERAL OIL & LAMPS

You cannot afford to pass these lamps by. They burn the safest oil on the market.

This ad dares buyers not to look at the lamps. It also makes promises about the oil's safety.

New Automatic Cameras

"You just press the button. We do all the rest."

Six new styles and sizes
For sale at all photo dealers

This ad promises to do all the work for the buyer.

Fizz

THE NEW DRINK

Refreshing

Invigorating

Satisfying

The seller tells what the new drink will do for the buyer.

Madison Cooking Stoves *and* Ranges

for wood or coal

Smart buyers choose Madison. One look will convince you that they are the best.

we guarantee satisfaction.

This ad uses flattery and promises satisfaction.

Ben Franklin's Words of Wisdom

from *Poor Richard's Almanack:*

Early to bed and early to rise makes a man healthy, wealthy, and wise.

There are no pains without gains.

Lost time is never found again.

Speak little, do much.

You may delay, but time will not.

The doors of wisdom are never shut.

One today is worth two tomorrows.

Well done is better than well said.

Strategy Planner

Step ❶ What is the author's purpose for writing?

☐ to tell a story **OR** ☐ to give information

☐ to entertain

Step ❷ What is your purpose for reading?

☐ for enjoyment **OR** ☐ for information

Step ❸ What type of story are you going to read?

☐ **fiction** **OR** ☐ **nonfiction**

Do the following:

- Identify the characters and settings.
- Think about what happens and when it happens.
- Use what you know to read new words.

Do the following:

- Read (more) slowly.
- Identify facts about real people or events.
- Use maps, diagrams, and pictures.
- Concentrate as you read.

Fluency: Phrasing and Accuracy

Listen to the pauses the reader makes.
Mark short pauses with one line (/).
Mark longer pauses with two lines (//).

Switch On, Switch Off

It's time to go to sleep. You go to your bedroom. The room is dark. You flip the switch on the wall. The light goes on.

You get into your pajamas. Just before you jump into bed, you flip down the switch. The light goes off. Flip up and the light goes on. Flip down and the light goes off. It seems like magic, but it's not magic at all. It's electricity!

Electricity is a form of energy. Energy is the power to do work. You have a lot of energy. Your energy lets you walk, run, throw a ball, ride a bike, and sometimes even clean your room!

Scoring Chart

Total Words Read in One Minute	Minus Words Missed	Total Words Read Correctly

A Letter About Electricity

Dear Enrique,

We made electricity in school today! We used a **magnet** and a piece of wire. First we made a **circuit** by coiling the wire and twisting its ends together. Then we pulled the magnet back and forth inside the coil. It made electricity!

Did you know that electricity is a form of **energy**? Everything is made up of tiny, tiny bits called **atoms**. The atoms have even tinier bits called **electrons** that move around inside of them. It's amazing!

Your friend,

Carlos

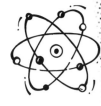

Conductor or Nonconductor?

Objects that allow electricity to flow through them are called *conductors*.
Objects that do not allow electricity to flow through them are called *nonconductors*.

Materials:

1 D-cell battery; 1 1.2-volt light bulb and base; 3 lengths of insulated, solid strand 18–22 gauge copper wire with one inch of insulation removed at each end; masking tape; objects and materials to test

Question: What materials conduct electricity?

1. Use the Hypothesis and Observation Chart to list what you will test. Predict whether the object will conduct electricity or not.

2. Connect the circuit as shown in the diagram below. Use masking tape to attach the wires to the battery.

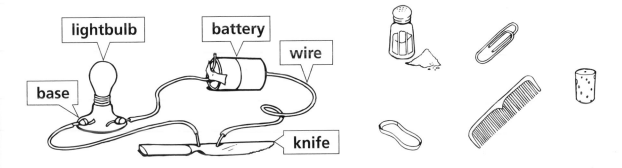

To test the circuit, touch the bare ends of the wires together. **HOLD THE COVERED PARTS OF THE WIRE ONLY. NEVER TOUCH THE BARE ENDS!**

3. Touch two places on the test object with the ends of the wires. Make sure to get good contact.
   - If the bulb lights up, the circuit is closed and the material is a conductor.
   - If the bulb does not light up, the circuit is open and the material is not a conductor.

4. Record the results for each test object or material in the chart.

Name _____ Date _____

Hypothesis and Observation Chart

Object / Material	Hypothesis		Observation	
	Will Conduct	**Will Not Conduct**	**Did Conduct**	**Did Not Conduct**

Energy Usage

You can spend a lot of money on energy to power things like light bulbs, ovens, and televisions. Switching to appliances and activities that use less energy can save money.

Look at the costs below. The energy to run these appliances might cost a little more or a little less in your area, but you can use these costs to make some comparisons.

4 incandescent light bulbs: $.04 per hour
4 compact fluorescent bulbs: $.01 per hour

Microwave oven: $.18 per hour
Electric oven: $.60 per hour
Electric rangetop burner: $.30 per hour

Window air conditioner: $.28 per hour
Central air conditioning: $.66 per hour
Electric fan: $.07 per hour

Color TV: $.05 per hour
Stereo: $.03 per hour
Computer: $.02 per hour
Board game: $0 per hour
Book: $0 per hour

Unit 6 | It's Electrifying!
© Hampton-Brown

67

Master 64
For use with TE pp. T363a–T363b

Glossary of Electrical Terms

battery (**bat**-u-rē) *noun* [L *battuere* beat] something that can supply electrical energy

circuit (**sur**-kut) *noun* [L *circuire* go around] the complete path of an electric current

closed circuit (klōzd **sur**-kut) *noun* a circuit in which current flows from the power source and back

conductor (kun-**duk**-tur) *noun* [L *conducere* act of leading] a material that allows electric current to flow through it

electrical energy (i-**lek**-tri-kul **en**-ur-jē) *noun* the energy provided by an electric current

electricity (i-lek-**tris**-ut-ē) *noun* [Gk *elektron, elektor* beaming sun] electric current or power

filament (**fil**-u-munt) *noun* [L *filare* spin] the coiled piece of wire inside a bulb that glows when electric current passes through it

fuse (fyūz) *noun* [L *fusus* pour, melt] a circuit safety device that contains a thin wire that melts and breaks when too much current passes through it

nonconductor (non-kun-**duk**-tur) *noun* [L *non* not + *conducere* act of leading] a material that does not allow electric current to flow through it

open circuit (ō-pun **sur**-kut) *noun* a circuit in which current cannot flow from the power source and back

switch (swich) *noun* a device used to open or close a circuit

volt (vōlt) *noun* [Alessandro *Volta*] the unit by which the strength of a battery or an electric current is measured

Pronunciation Key	
ā	cake
ē	key
ī	bike
ō	goat
ū	fruit
yū	mule

Unit 6 | It's Electrifying!
© Hampton-Brown

68

Master 65
For use with TE pp. T365a–T365b

March Costs

Pretend that fifty people from your town want to attend a Civil Rights March in
Washington, D.C. How long will it take to get there and how much will it cost?

- The speed of the bus is 300 miles per day.
- A bus for 50 people costs $500 per day.
- Meals for 50 people cost an average of $1,500 each day.
- Hotel rooms for 50 people cost an average of $1,750 per night.

Problem A: How long will the trip take?

1. Write the number of miles from your town to Washington, D.C.	_____ miles
2. Divide the number of miles by the speed of the bus. This is the number of days the trip will take.	_____ days

Problem B: How much will the trip cost?

1. Write the number of days the trip will take. (from step 2 above)	_____ days
2. Multiply the number of days by the bus cost per day.	$
3. Multiply the number of days by the average cost of meals per day.	$
4. Multiply the number of nights by the average cost of hotel rooms per night.	$
5. Add steps 2, 3, and 4 to find the cost of the trip each way.	$

Prediction Chart

What I know about the character	What I think will happen

Role-Play a Conversation

Use this script to perform a role-play.

Blooming Mary: My flowers have been watered already. Are you lost, child?

'Tricia Ann: No, Ma'am, I just wish my grandmother was here to help me get to Someplace Special.

Blooming Mary: You can't get there by yourself?

'Tricia Ann: It's too hard. I need my grandmother.

Blooming Mary: I believe your granny <u>is</u> here, just as my granny is here with me even as I speak. Listen close. Tell me what you hear.

Mama Frances: You are somebody, a human being. You are no better, no worse than anybody else in this world. Getting someplace special is not an easy route, but don't think about quitting. Just keep walking straight ahead, and you'll make it.

'Tricia Ann: You were right, Ma'am. Mama Frances is here, and she wouldn't want me to turn back.

Blooming Mary: So, you aren't lost after all.

'Tricia Ann: No, Ma'am, I'm not.

A Letter from 'Tricia Ann

Dear Mayor,

Peace Fountain is one of my **favorite** places, but I can't sit on the benches there. I am **determined** to change that. Everyone should be able to enjoy that **special** place. All **public** places should be **welcoming** to everybody.

Please, Mr. Mayor, change the laws. Give **protection** to every person's rights. Make Nashville a better city.

Sincerely,

'Tricia Ann Johnson

P.S. I would love to have a **conversation** with you about ways to make our laws fair.

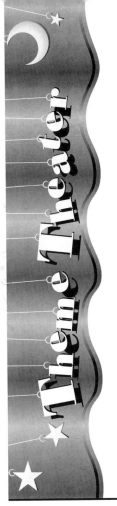

Theme Theater

Going Someplace Special

Setting

The play takes place in three locations in Nashville, Tennessee, in the 1950s.

Cast of Characters

Tricia Ann   Mama Frances

Narrator   Mrs. Grannell

Blooming Mary   People on bus

Scene 3: The Garden

Tricia Ann and Blooming Mary on stage.

Tricia Ann (crying): I'm going home.

Mary: Are you lost, child?

Tricia Ann: No, Ma'am, I just wish my grandmother was here to help me get to Someplace Special.

Mary: You can't get there by yourself?

Tricia Ann: It's too hard. I need my grandmother.

Mary: I believe your granny is here, just as my granny is here with me even as I speak. Listen close. Tell me what you hear.

Mama Frances (*offstage*): You are somebody, a human being. You are no better, no worse than anybody else in this world. Getting someplace special is not an easy route, but don't think about quitting. Just keep walking straight ahead, and you'll make it.

Tricia Ann: You were right, Ma'am. Mama Frances is here, and she wouldn't want me to turn back.

End of play.

Unit 7 | Going Places with Patricia McKissack
© Hampton-Brown

73

Master 70
For use with TE pp. T403a–T403b

Scene 1: At Home

'Tricia Ann and Mama Frances are on stage.

'Tricia Ann (*bursting with excitement*): Mama Frances, may I go to Someplace Special by myself today?

Mama Frances smiles and shakes her head.

'Tricia Ann: Pretty please? I know where to get off the bus and what streets to take. Pretty please with marshmallows on top?

Mama Frances (*tying the sash of 'Tricia Ann's dress*): I don't know if I'm ready to turn you loose in the world. Going off alone is a mighty big step.

'Tricia Ann (*leaps across the floor*): I'm ready. See what a big step I can make?

Mama Frances (*chuckles*): You'll be careful and remember what I've told you, right?

'Tricia Ann: I will. So you're saying I can go?

Mama Frances: Yes . . . but you better go before I change my mind.

'Tricia Ann blows a kiss and exits.

Scene 2: On the Bus

'Tricia Ann gets onto a nearly full bus and sees the Jim Crow sign.

Mama Frances (*offstage*): Those signs can tell us where to sit, but they can't tell us what to think.

Enter Mrs. Grannell.

'Tricia Ann (*takes a seat in the back*): I'm going to think about going Someplace Special.

Narrator: Mrs. Grannell, Mama Frances's friend from the sewing circle, climbs on board. 'Tricia Ann notices that there are no seats left behind the Jim Crow sign.

'Tricia Ann (*stands up and gives Mrs. Grannell her seat*): It's not fair!

Mrs. Grannell: No, but that's the way it is, honey.

'Tricia Ann (*puzzled*): I don't understand why.

'Tricia Ann realizes it's her stop, starts to exit.

Mrs. Grannell: Walk with pride!

'Tricia Ann exits.

Getting to Someplace Special

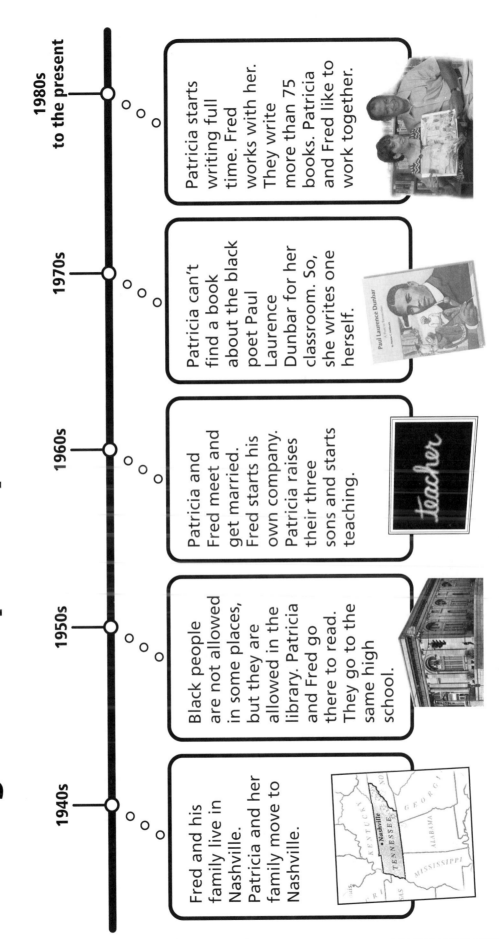

1940s

Fred and his family live in Nashville. Patricia and her family move to Nashville.

1950s

Black people are not allowed in some places, but they are allowed in the library. Patricia and Fred go there to read. They go to the same high school.

1960s

Patricia and Fred meet and get married. Fred starts his own company. Patricia raises their three sons and starts teaching.

1970s

Patricia can't find a book about the black poet Paul Laurence Dunbar for her classroom. So, she writes one herself.

1980s to the present

Patricia starts writing full time. Fred works with her. They write more than 75 books. Patricia and Fred like to work together.

Fluency: Phrasing and Accuracy

Listen to the pauses the reader makes.
Mark short pauses with one line (/).
Mark longer pauses with two lines (//).

Getting to Someplace Special

While I was teaching, I took my first steps toward becoming a writer. Once again, the library played a significant role in my life. Let me explain. Before I was a parent or teacher, I was a listener. Mother recited the poetry of Paul Laurence Dunbar to me when I was a little girl. "Little Brown Baby" was my favorite poem. I never got tired of hearing it. Later, I taught it to my sons.

As a teacher, I wanted to share Dunbar's life and poetry with my students. When I went to the library to check out a biography of him, I couldn't find one for young readers. In fact, in 1971, there weren't a lot of books about African Americans in any of the libraries I visited. Since I needed a biography of Paul Laurence Dunbar, I decided to write it myself. That was easier said than done. I'd never written a book before.

Scoring Chart

Total Words Read in One Minute	Minus Words Missed	Total Words Read Correctly

A Letter to Patricia McKissack

Dear Ms. McKissack,

Your book Flossie and the Fox **inspired** me to make up a story about a clever boy and a bear. My friends loved it.

I wrote a historical fiction story, too, but it wasn't as real as yours. Your husband's research really **makes a difference**. You two have a winning **partnership**!

My teacher **encourages** me to become a writer. I **respect** her opinion, but my friends think I should be a comedian. I think I have a **compromise**: I'll be a writer who writes funny stories!

Sincerely,

Dion Walters

Name _____ Date _____

Multicultural Calendar

Choose two holidays that happen in the same month from different cultures.
Draw a picture for each holiday.
Write the name of each holiday, its date, and its culture.
Tell about each holiday.

Month: _____

Holiday: _____   Holiday: _____

Date: _____   Date: _____

Culture: _____   Culture: _____

_____   _____

_____   _____

_____   _____

_____   _____

Self-Monitoring Card

Get Unstuck!

I don't understand _____

_____

I think I'm stuck because _____

_____

To get unstuck, I will try _____

_____

Now I understand _____

_____

Name	Date

Get Unstuck!

I don't understand _____

_____

I think I'm stuck because _____

_____

To get unstuck, I will try _____

_____

Now I understand _____

_____

Name	Date

A Letter to Juanito

Dear Juanito,

Soon it will be time to **harvest** the grapes in the valley. I am glad that you are going to school, but I will miss seeing you in **camp**.

My parents think it is time to quit doing **migrant** work and **settle down**. It has been hard to change schools so much. I miss my friends each time we **move on**.

Please write and tell me how you like your school and your neighborhood. Who knows? Maybe we could come and live near you!

Your friend,

Carlos

Theme Theater Props

Unit 8 | We the People
© Hampton-Brown

81

Master 78
For use with TE pp. T457a–T457b

Coming to America

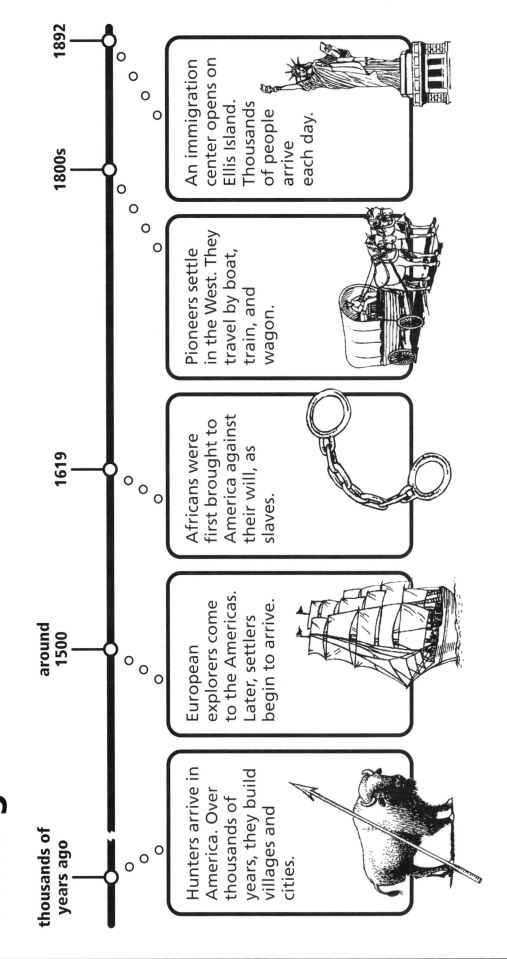

thousands of years ago

Hunters arrive in America. Over thousands of years, they build villages and cities.

around 1500

European explorers come to the Americas. Later, settlers begin to arrive.

1619

Africans were first brought to America against their will, as slaves.

1800s

Pioneers settle in the West. They travel by boat, train, and wagon.

1892

An immigration center opens on Ellis Island. Thousands of people arrive each day.

Glossary of Social Studies Terms

country of origin (kun-trē uv **or**-u-jun) *noun* the land of a person's birth

culture (**kul**-chur) *noun* [L *cultura* cultivation, worship] the beliefs and customs of a group of people

ethnic group (**eth**-nik gryūp) *noun* [Gk *ethnos* nation] a group of people who share the same race or nationality

heritage (**hair**-u-tij) *noun* [L *hereditare* inherit] traditions, ideas, or language from an ancestor

homeland (**hōm**-land) *noun* a person's native land

immigrant (**im**-u-grunt) *noun* [L *im* into + *migra* depart] a person who comes to a country to live

immigrate (**im**-u-grāt) *verb* [L *migra* depart] to come to a new country to live

migrate (**mī**-grāt) *verb* [L *migra* depart] to move from one country or place to another

migrant (**mī**-grunt) *adjective* [L *migra* depart] often traveling or moving to find work

pioneer (**pī**-u-nēr) *noun* [OF *paonier* foot soldier] one of the first people to explore and settle in an area

settlement (**set**-ul-munt) noun [OE *setl* sitting place] a place where settlers live and stay; a village

settler (**set**-lur) noun [OE *setl* sitting place] a person who moves to a new region to live

Pronunciation Key	
ā	cake
ē	key
ī	bike
ō	goat
ū	fruit
yū	mule

A Letter to Betsy Maestro

Dear Ms. Maestro,

I liked reading about how much **immigrants** have added to American **culture**.

Since I'm the **descendant** of **pioneers** and **settlers**, it made me see how brave my **distant relatives** were.

I would like to become an **explorer** someday. I want to explore planets out in space!

Your fan,

Julia Ramirez

Name _____   Date _____

Comparison Chart

Use this chart to compare characteristics of different immigrant groups.

Immigrant Group	Where did they come from?	How did they get to the U.S.?	Why did they come?	When did most of them arrive?	What did they bring from their culture?

Unit 8 | We the People
© Hampton-Brown

85

Master 82
For use with TE pp. T487a–T487b

Avenues
Writing Project Masters

Features of a Personal Narrative

Read "A Good Luck Valentine."
Check the box if the personal narrative has the feature.
Write the details.

Features	Does It Have the Feature?
The personal narrative tells a true story. It tells about something that happened to the writer.	☑ *Yes. The girl writes about her first Valentine's Day.*
The personal narrative has a beginning, middle, and end.	☐
It uses the words *I*, *me*, and *my*.	☐
It includes order words to tell when things happened.	☐
It includes describing words to tell how the writer felt.	☐

Name _____   Date _____

Writing Project

Writing Prompt

Write a personal narrative about a good time you have
shared with a family member. Describe your feelings about it.

❶ Think of Ideas

What good times have you had with your family?
What was special about those times? Write your ideas.

Good Times

1. cooking a birthday meal
2. _____
   _____
3. _____
   _____
4. _____
   _____
5. _____
   _____

❷ Choose a Topic

Choose one idea for the topic of your
personal narrative. Circle it.

Plan Your Narrative

**Write the title of your personal narrative. Then plan the parts.
Use a story map.**

Title: _____

```
┌─────────────────────────────────────────────────────┐
│                     Beginning:                       │
│                                                       │
│                                                       │
│                                                       │
└─────────────────────────────────────────────────────┘
                          ↓
┌─────────────────────────────────────────────────────┐
│                       Middle:                        │
│                                                       │
│                                                       │
│                                                       │
└─────────────────────────────────────────────────────┘
                          ↓
┌─────────────────────────────────────────────────────┐
│                        End:                          │
│                                                       │
│                                                       │
│                                                       │
└─────────────────────────────────────────────────────┘
```

Good Writing Trait: Focus and Coherence

	Are the Ideas Related?	Is the Writing Complete?
4 Wow! You have it!	▢ All of the ideas are about one topic.	▢ There is a beginning and an end. ▢ All of the details in the middle are important.
3 Good job!	▢ Most of the ideas are about one topic.	▢ There is a beginning and an end. ▢ Most of the details in the middle are important.
2 Not quite	▢ There are many ideas that don't go together. It is hard to tell what the writing is all about.	▢ The writing has a beginning or an end, but it doesn't have both. ▢ Some of the details in the middle don't belong there.
1 Try again!	▢ The ideas don't go together. I can't tell what the writing is really about.	▢ The writing does not have a beginning. ▢ The writing does not have an end.

Write a Draft

Start writing your draft below.
Keep writing on a separate sheet of paper.

Title: _____

Start with a title.

Write a good beginning.

Revise

Read the personal narrative. Make changes to improve the focus. Write a stronger beginning. Take out ideas that don't belong.

Revising Marks

Mark	Meaning
∧	Add.
___ℯ	Take out.
∧ℯ	Change to this.
↻	Move to here.

A Birthday Treat

It is my tenth birthday. My Aunt Carmen cooks a special Dominican dish just for me. Aunt Carmen has red hair. It is called *asopao*, a delicious type of stew made with seafood and rice. Aunt Carmen says that eating the *asopao* reminds her of growing up in the Dominican Republic.

I want to learn how to make *asopao*, too. First, Aunt Carmen and I go to the market. I see my friend Elisa at the market. buy all the ingredients. Back home in the kitchen, Aunt Carmen shows me how to prepare the *asopao*. When the *asopao* is done, my whole family enjoys it.

Think About Focus and Coherence

❏ Are all the ideas about one topic?

❏ Is there a beginning and an end?

❏ Are all of the details in the middle important?

Edit and Proofread

Read the rest of the story. Check for errors in capitalization, spelling, and punctuation. Make sure that the subjects and verbs agree. Use Proofreading Marks.

One week later, it's Aunt Carmen's birthday. She seem a little homesick for the dominican republic. I think she needs a speshial surprise So my dad and I go to the market. Then i fix a huge pot of *asopao*. After the meal, Aunt Carmen huggs me. She says it are the best *asopao* she have ever tasted. I feels very proud.

Proofreading Marks

Mark	Meaning
∧	Add.
∧	Add a comma.
⊙	Add a period.
≡	Capitalize.
◯	Check spelling.
/	Make lowercase.
⟋	Take out.

Features of a Report

Read "Moving."
Check the box if the report has the feature.
Write the details.

Features	Does It Have the Feature?
The report gives facts about a topic.	☑ Yes. It says your spine has 33 bones that bend so you can move.
Pictures and diagrams explain important information.	☐
The report has a title and an introduction. They tell what the report is about.	☐
Each paragraph has a topic sentence that tells one main idea about the topic.	☐
Details in the paragraph tell more about its main idea.	☐
The report has a conclusion. It sums up the report.	☐

Writing Project

Writing Prompt

Write a report about a way to stay healthy.
Give information about why this idea is important.

1 Think of Ideas

What do you know about staying healthy?
Write your ideas.

Staying Healthy
1. exercise
2. _____
   _____
3. _____
   _____
4. _____
   _____
5. _____
   _____

2 Choose a Topic

Choose one idea for the topic of your report.
Circle it.

Plan Your Paragraphs

Write the topic of your report.
Then plan your paragraphs.
Use the diagram.

Topic: _____

Paragraph 1:

Paragraph 2:

Good Writing Trait: Organization

	Is the Whole Thing Organized?	Does the Writing Flow?
4 Wow! You have it!	☐ The writing is very well-organized. It fits the writer's purpose.	☐ The writing is very smooth. Each idea flows into the next one.
3 Good job!	☐ The writing is organized. It fits the writer's purpose.	☐ The writing is pretty smooth. There are only a few places where it jumps around.
2 Not quite	☐ The writing is organized, but it doesn't fit the writer's purpose.	☐ The writing jumps from one idea to another idea, but I can follow it a little.
1 Try again!	☐ The writing is not organized. Maybe the writer forgot to use a chart to plan.	☐ I can't tell what the writer wants to say.

Write a Draft

Draw a diagram for your report.
Then start writing your report below.
Keep writing on a separate sheet of paper.

Title: _____

> **Start with a topic sentence.** _____

_____

_____

_____

_____

_____

_____

Revise

Read the report. Make changes to improve the organization.

Revising Marks

Mark	Meaning
$\wedge$	Add.
⤳	Take out.
⤳	Change to this.
⟳	Move to here.

Exercise

Aerobic exercise brings oxygen to your heart. Exercise is good for your body in many ways. Aerobic activities include swimming, jogging, biking, and dancing. These activities all help your heart become stronger and a little bit bigger. Then your heart can pump more blood through your body. You won't get as tired when you exercise!

Exercise helps your muscles. Strong muscles help protect you from injury when you exercise. Aerobic exercise brings oxygen to your muscles and makes them stronger. You can exercise longer.

Think About Organization

❑ Is the writing well-organized? Does it fit the writer's purpose?

❑ Does everything make sense?

❑ Is the writing smooth? Does one idea flow into the next one?

Edit and Proofread

Read the rest of the report. Check for errors in capitalization, spelling, and punctuation. Make sure that pronouns are used correctly. Use Proofreading Marks.

How does exercise help you stay flexible Stretching exercises make their muscles longer. longer muscles help you bend and stretch beter Gymnastics karate, and ballet are good activities for staying flexible. Staying flexible means you are less likely to get injured when we exercise

Proofreading Marks

Mark	Meaning
∧	Add.
⩞	Add a comma.
⊙	Add a period.
≡	Capitalize.
◯	Check spelling.
/	Make lowercase.
⟋ℯ	Take out.

Features of a Tall Tale

Read "The Bunyans."
Check the box if the tale has the feature.
Write the details.

Features	Does It Have the Feature?
The tall tale has exaggerated details.	☑ Yes. It says that Paul was taller than a redwood tree.
The main character has special powers or great strength.	☐
The writer uses funny, colorful words.	☐
The tall tale explains how something came to be.	☐

Writing Project

Writing Prompt

**Write a tall tale to explain how a landform was made.
Use exaggerated details in your writing.**

1 Think of Ideas

What landforms do you know?
Write your ideas.

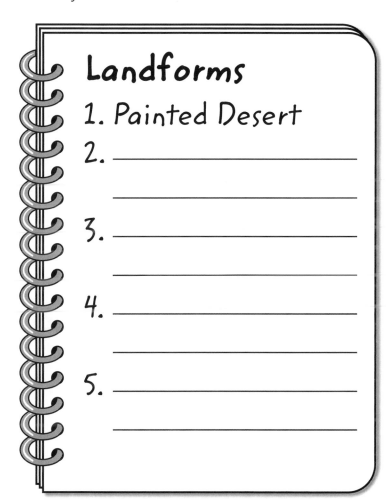

Landforms
1. Painted Desert
2. _____
   _____
3. _____
   _____
4. _____
   _____
5. _____
   _____

2 Choose a Topic

Choose one idea for the topic of your tall tale.
Circle it.

Plan Your Tall Tale

Make a web about your main character.
Then write notes about the landform he or she created.

Title: _____

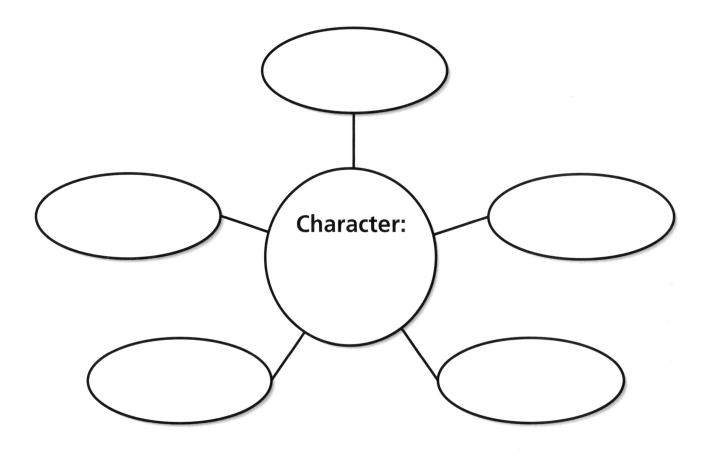

Character:

_____

_____

_____

_____

_____

Good Writing Trait: Voice

	Does the writing sound real?	Do the words fit the purpose and audience?
4 **Wow! You have it!**	☐ The writing shows who the writer is. ☐ The writer seems to be talking right to me.	☐ The writer uses words that really fit the purpose and audience.
3 **Good job!**	☐ The writing shows who the writer is. ☐ The writer does a good job sounding real.	☐ The writer uses good words for the purpose and audience.
2 **Not quite**	☐ It's hard to tell who the writer is. ☐ The writer doesn't seem to be talking to me.	☐ The writer uses some words that fit the purpose and audience.
1 **Try again!**	☐ I can't tell who the writer is. ☐ The writer doesn't seem to care.	☐ The words don't fit the purpose and audience.

Write a Draft

Draw a picture of your main character. Then start writing
your tall tale. Keep writing on a separate sheet of paper.

Title: _____ **Start with a title.**

Introduce your character. _____

_____

_____

_____

_____

_____

_____

_____

Revise

Read the tall tale. Make changes to improve the voice. Replace the underlined words with more interesting words.

Revising Marks

Mark	Meaning
∧	Add.
⌐	Take out.
∧⌐	Change to this.
⟳	Move to here.

Pee Wee Gets a Hobby

Pee Wee's life was not very interesting. Everyone else in his family had a good hobby. His father made mountains on Mondays. Pee Wee's mother wrestled rattlesnakes on weekends. She said it made her feel young. His sister liked to capture crocodiles and brush their teeth. She didn't want the animals to get cavities in their nice teeth. Poor Pee Wee. He didn't have anything fun to do.

Pee Wee was a short boy. He was only as tall as a giraffe, which is short in his family. He didn't like animals very much. He liked to draw, though. One day his mom gave him some paint and a paintbrush. He was pretty excited. He couldn't wait to begin.

He painted the walls. He painted the ceilings. He painted the furniture. He painted the windows. He painted the TV. He was just about to paint the dog, when his mom came in.

Think About Voice

❑ Does the writer have a special way of saying things?

❑ Does the writer seem to care about the ideas?

❑ Does the writer use interesting words and phrases? Do the words fit the purpose and the audience?

Edit and Proofread

Read the rest of the tall tale. Check for errors in capitalization, spelling, and punctuation. Use Proofreading Marks.

His mom got really mad when she saw all the paint. Mom said, "Pee Wee! You stop that right now. Go outside, young man!"

Pee wee did go outside. his Mom thought he would stop. But he did not stop painting. He just couldn't. He had a hobby that he liked. No one or nothing would get in his way. He painted the driveway. He painted the trees, and he just kept going. He painted all the rocks for hundreds of miles around. He went up mountains and into canyons, even the grand Canyon. He painted everything.

And that's how the Painted Desert and Rainbow Forest in arizona came to be. You can thank Pee Wee for that pretty part of the world.

Proofreading Marks

Mark	Meaning
∧	Add.
⌄	Add a comma.
⊙	Add a period.
≡	Capitalize.
◯	Check spelling.
/	Make lowercase.
⌿	Take out.

Features of a Persuasive Letter

Read "Fair or Unfair."
Check the box if the writing has the feature.
Write the details.

Features	Does It Have the Feature?
The persuasive writing gives an opinion.	☑ Yes. The person thinks the tax on tea is unfair.
Good reasons support the opinion.	☐
The writer uses persuasive words to get readers to think a certain way.	☐
The letter tells what action readers should take.	☐

Writing Project

Writing Prompt

**Write a persuasive letter to make a change in your school.
Include reasons for your opinion.**

1 Think of Ideas

What changes would make your school
a better place? Write your ideas.

School Changes

1. International Day
   celebration

2. _____

   _____

3. _____

   _____

4. _____

   _____

5. _____

   _____

2 Choose a Topic

Choose one idea for your persuasive letter.
Circle it.

Plan Your Letter

Plan your persuasive letter.
Use the diagram.

Opinion:

_____

_____

Reasons:

1. _____

_____

2. _____

_____

3. _____

_____

Action to take:

_____

_____

Name _____ Date _____

Good Writing Trait: Development of Ideas

	Is the writing interesting?	How well do you understand the ideas?
4 **Wow! You have it!**	☐ The writer has thought about the topic carefully. ☐ The ideas are presented in a very interesting way.	☐ The writing answered all of my questions. There were enough details to help me understand.
3 **Good job!**	☐ The writer has thought about the topic. ☐ The ideas are presented in an interesting way.	☐ The writing answered most of my questions. There were enough details to help me understand.
2 **Not quite**	☐ The writer doesn't seem to have thought about the topic very much. ☐ The writing is OK, but not interesting.	☐ I have some questions that were not answered.
1 **Try again!**	☐ The writer doesn't seem to have thought about the topic at all. ☐ The ideas are presented in a boring way.	☐ I have a lot of questions. The writing didn't tell me enough.

Write a Draft

Start writing your persuasive letter below.
Keep writing on a separate sheet of paper.

Dear _____ : **Write the greeting.**

_____

_____

_____

_____

_____

_____

_____

_____

_____

_____

_____

_____

_____

Revise

Read the persuasive letter.
Revise it to develop the ideas in more depth.

Revising Marks

Mark	Meaning
∧	Add.
⟋	Take out.
∧	Change to this.
⟲	Move to here.

Dear Mr. Hanson:

I think our school should start a celebration. We can call it International Day. The celebration can focus on all the cultures we have in our school. We can have things from different cultures.

Many of the students at our school come from different places. I think we would all enjoy sharing our cultures with others. It would also be a chance to learn about each other's cultures.

We can invite family members. We can get them involved in our school.

Think About Development of Ideas

❏ Has the writer thought about the topic carefully?

❏ Does the writing cover the topic fully?

❏ Are the ideas presented in an interesting way?

❏ Are there enough reasons to support the opinion?

Edit and Proofread

Read the rest of the persuasive letter.
Check for errors in capitalization, spelling,
and punctuation. Use Proofreading Marks.

Please set aside a day when the hole school can

participate, I volunteer to get a group of student, teachers

and familys together to plan the first Intrenational Day. If

we start now we could celebreat international Day before

the end of the school year. I think International day will be a

great day for everyone Don't you agree.

Sincerely

Chou Feng

Chou Feng

Proofreading Marks

Mark	Meaning
∧	Add.
∧•	Add a comma.
⊙	Add a period.
≡	Capitalize.
◯	Check spelling.
/	Make lowercase.
⌒e	Take out.

Avenues
Student Writing Samples

Read this story.
Think about how well it is written.
Give it a score. Circle the number.

Focus and Coherence
Score
1   2   3   4

The Field Trip

One day at school, Hector's teacher held up a small plastic dinosaur. It was a brown Brontosaurus. The teacher said the dinosaur was a clue about their next field trip. She wanted the students to guess where they might be going.

Everyone named a different place. No one guessed the right place until Tina said, "Are we going to the Science Museum? I know there's a new dinosaur exhibit there."

That was the right guess. The next week, the class got on the bus and rode to the Science Museum. They had studied dinosaurs in books, but here was their chance to see life-size models!

At the museum, the class had a guide who knew all about dinosaurs. He let the students wander around the exhibit and look at the models. Then he gave a talk about each one.

When the guide was finished talking, the students had a chance to ask questions. Hector wanted to know how fast Tyrannosaurus rex could run. Tina wanted to know how big Stegosaurus' eggs were. Everyone had a question, and the guide answered them all. Then it was time to go back to school.

The next day, the students thanked their teacher for the field trip. They told her they had learned a lot in one day. Hector wanted to know where they would go for their next field trip. The teacher just smiled and held up a starfish.

Evaluate Writing Samples
© Hampton-Brown

118

Master 111
For use with TE pp. T62d–T62e

Read this story.
Think about how well it is written.
Give it a score. Circle the number.

Focus and Coherence
Score
1   2   3   4

Pet Day

Sakura put her cat, Grumpy, in the cat carrier. It was Pet Day at school. Sakura was so happy about bringing Grumpy to school. She knew that he would have a good time.

Sakura thought that Grumpy was a better pet than a dog. Dogs were noisy and liked to run around chasing squirrels. Grumpy was a nice, quiet pet. He liked to eat tuna fish.

Sakura's mom drove Sakura and Grumpy to school. Sakura's friends brought their pets, too. Manuel had a fish in a small tank. Josh had a hamster. Lena had a dog on a leash. The dog was barking!

At the end of the day, Sakura's mom was going to pick up Sakura and Grumpy. Mr. Lee, her teacher, wrote the students' names on the board. He said they would share their pets in that order. Sakura's name was near the end.

The students shared their pets. When it was Sakura's turn, she opened the cat carrier. Grumpy jumped right out and ran toward Lena's barking dog! The dog got away from Lena and chased Grumpy around the room!

Now all the students and Mr. Lee chased Grumpy and Lena's dog. At last, Mr. Lee caught Grumpy. He handed the cat to Sakura. Lena got her dog back. Then the bell rang. Everyone was glad that school was over and the pets could go home.

STUDENT WRITING SAMPLE

Read this story.
Think about how well it is written.
Give it a score. Circle the number.

Focus and Coherence
Score
1   2   3   4

The Science Fair

Every year, Todd's school has a Science Fair. This year there will be a Science Fair, too. Todd has to think of a science project. Each fifth-grader must have a project in the Science Fair.

Todd likes science, but his favorite subject is reading. He likes to read biographies of sports heroes. He also likes to read books of riddles. Then he asks his friends the riddles. He can usually fool his friends with them.

Todd thinks he might do his science project on the rain forest. He could make a diorama with little clay models of the animals who live there. He could tell people ways to save the rain forests. Todd will ask his teacher if that is a good idea.

Todd's teacher is Ms. Hill. She teaches science three days a week. Right now, the class is learning about the planets and stars. They might take a field trip to an observatory.

The Science Fair is three weeks away. Ms. Hill likes Todd's idea about the rain forest. She tells him to get started. He goes to the library. He uses encyclopedias and the Internet. In three weeks, Todd's rain forest project is finished.

The Science Fair is in the gym. The basketball team plays games in the gym. Todd's rain forest project is set up on a table. Ms. Hill and the other teachers look at it. They tell Todd he did a good job.

Evaluate Writing Samples
© Hampton-Brown

120

Master 113
For use with TE pp. T62d–T62e

Read this story.
Think about how well it is written.
Give it a score. Circle the number.

Focus and Coherence
Score

1   2   3   4

The Car Wash

Ishana's school had a car wash to raise money for new computers. The fourth-grade students washed cars on Saturday. That was last Saturday. Ishana is in the fourth grade.

Some of the parents and teachers helped. They got hoses and buckets. They got sponges and soap. A lot of adults are usually busy on Saturdays. They helped wash and dry cars all day. The car wash cost five dollars for each car.

The school needed new computers. There was only one computer in the library and it was very old. Also, it was too hard to share one computer. The teachers wanted to have a new computer in each classroom. The parents said, "Let's have a car wash. We can raise money for the new computers."

Some parents wanted to collect cans and bottles. They said it was a good way to get money. And it helped save the earth because it was recycling, too. Some parents didn't like that idea. They said there was no room at the school to keep all those cans and bottles.

Last year, the school had a bake sale. The bake sale was in the cafeteria. The bake sale raised money for library books. Some of the parents and students baked cakes, cookies, and pies. Ishana baked brownies. Most people bought chocolate chip cookies. The bake sale raised a lot of money, so the library got a lot of new books.

Evaluate Writing Samples
© Hampton-Brown

121

Master 114
For use with TE pp. T12d–T12e

STUDENT WRITING SAMPLE

Read this report.
Think about how well it is written.
Give it a score. Circle the number.

Organization
Score
1   2   3   4

Volcanoes

A volcano starts as an opening in the Earth's crust. The opening is called a vent. Hot, melted rock forms deep below the Earth's surface. The melted rock is called magma. It pushes through the vent in the Earth's crust. When the magma reaches the air, it is called lava. The lava pours out and starts to cool off. It forms a cone, or mountain. Each time the volcano erupts, the lava builds up and the volcano gets bigger.

Some of the world's volcanoes are above sea level, but most are below the sea. Some islands, such as the Hawaiian Islands, are actually the tops of undersea volcanoes.

Volcanoes can be active, dormant, or extinct. An active volcano erupts often. A dormant volcano does not erupt a lot. An extinct volcano has stopped erupting.

Active volcanoes can be dangerous to people. Lava flows and ash can damage or destroy property. Sometimes volcanoes cause earthquakes or giant sea waves called tsunamis. These natural disasters can injure or kill people.

Today scientists try to predict when a volcano will erupt. They measure small earthquakes caused by moving magma. They measure gas that is released when the magma gets near the Earth's surface. Scientists watch volcanoes closely so they can warn people to get away.

Evaluate Writing Samples
© Hampton-Brown

122

Master 115
For use with TE pp. T182d–T182e

STUDENT WRITING SAMPLE

Read this report.
Think about how well it is written.
Give it a score. Circle the number.

Earthquakes

The Earth's crust is made up of huge sections called plates. The plates are made of rock. The plates are always moving. They move very slowly. Sometimes the plates move sideways and sometimes they move up and down.

The crack between two plates is called a fault. Most earthquakes happen along faults, when two plates run into each other. This makes waves of energy. The waves travel through the ground, making it shake. I was in an earthquake once. It was scary!

The San Andreas fault is in California. This fault is more than 800 miles long. In some places, it is more than ten miles deep.

Every day there are thousands of earthquakes around the world. Most are so small that no one notices them. Scientists measure earthquakes with special equipment. They give each earthquake a number on the Richter scale. Charles Richter developed the Richter scale in 1935. Richter worked at the California Institute of Technology. The number tells the strength of the earthquake. People can't feel an earthquake that measures 0 on the scale, but they can feel one that is 4 or higher.

Earthquakes, hurricanes, and other disasters happen all over the world. Earthquakes can do a lot of damage. They can knock down buildings and cause landslides. They are one of nature's most powerful forces.

Evaluate Writing Samples
© Hampton-Brown

123

Master 116
For use with TE pp. T120d–T120e

Read this report.
Think about how well it is written.
Give it a score. Circle the number.

Organization
Score

1   2   3   4

Oceans

Where are the oceans? Why do fish live in the oceans? The oceans cover about 75% of the Earth's surface. The five major oceans are the Pacific Ocean, the Atlantic Ocean, the Indian Ocean, the Arctic Ocean, and the Southern Ocean. The deepest part of any ocean is in the Pacific. It is the Mariana Trench, and it is almost seven miles deep.

The largest animal in the world lives in the ocean. It is the blue whale. It is the largest animal of all, but other large animals are elephants and bears. Sharks, tuna, and seahorses live in the ocean. Plants such as seaweed and algae live in the ocean, too.

Some plants that live in the ocean have roots. Other plants float without roots. The plants with roots live near the surface of the ocean. They need sunlight to grow. The most common types of ocean plants are called phytoplankton. They have no roots, and they float right near the top of the ocean.

The oceans are salty because rainwater falls on the land. The rainwater takes salt from the rocks and the soil. Then the salt is carried into the oceans. Ocean water is made up of only a little salt.

Are there waves in the oceans? Most of the waves are caused by wind. It pushes the water up into waves. Sometimes earthquakes, volcanoes, or landslides cause waves. Of course, there are earthquakes and volcanoes on land, too.

Evaluate Writing Samples
© Hampton-Brown

124

Master 117
For use with TE pp. T182d–T182e

STUDENT WRITING SAMPLE

Read this report.
Think about how well it is written.
Give it a score. Circle the number.

Organization
Score

1   2   3   4

The Solar System

The Earth is the third closest planet to the Sun. The Earth moves around the Sun in a big loop. The solar system is made up of nine planets and the Sun. All the planets move around the Sun. The Sun is the center of the solar system. There are 365 days in one year. The Earth moves 365 days to make one full loop around the Sun.

The other planets in the solar system are Mercury, Venus, Mars, Jupiter, Saturn, Neptune, Uranus, and Pluto. The planets orbit the Sun. The inner planets are Mercury, Venus, Earth, and Mars. They orbit close to the Sun. The outer planets are Jupiter, Saturn, Uranus, Neptune, and Pluto. They orbit far away from the Sun. The farthest planet from the Sun is Pluto.

The inner planets are made mostly of rock and metal. Pluto also is mostly rocky. The outer planets are made up mostly of gases. Some spin slowly, and some spin fast. Some other things in the solar system are comets. Comets are small and icy. They move around the Sun. They have long tails and are very small. Mercury is the planet that moves the fastest.

Asteroids are like small planets. They orbit the Sun. Meteoroids are small pieces of rock or metal. They come from comets or asteroids. There are satellites in nature. And there are satellites made by humans in space. There are more than planets in the solar system.

Evaluate Writing Samples
© Hampton-Brown

125

Master 118
For use with TE pp. T120d–T120e

STUDENT WRITING SAMPLE

Read this story.
Think about how well it is written.
Give it a score. Circle the number.

Development of Ideas
Score

| 1 | 2 | 3 | 4 |

The Day the Sky Turned Green

"Boy, it sure is warm. It's like summer!" my mom said one day in March. Suddenly the sky seemed too dark. My mother told us to come inside right away. There was a tornado warning. I looked over the flat land around us. All I saw was that the dark sky had turned a strange color. "Green?" I said to myself. "I didn't know the sky could be green."

When we were all inside, Mom made us go to the basement. She brought bottled water, snacks, flashlights, and a radio. We crawled under the dusty stairs and waited. The world seemed silent. I could hear my little sister breathing next to me. I put my arm around her so she wouldn't be scared.

Then we heard a loud roar. It sounded like a train was coming! Suddenly we could feel the house shaking above us. The roaring got louder and louder. I thought it would never stop. Then we heard banging and crashing, as though the whole house was coming apart. My sister screamed. I did, too. The terrible sounds scared us all.

Within minutes, the roar died down. The tornado was going away. We could a hear a few small things rolling around upstairs.

When Mom said it was safe, we crept upstairs and opened the door. We stood there, looking up at the bright blue sky. We hugged and laughed and cried. Our roof was gone, but we were all okay!

Evaluate Writing Samples
© Hampton-Brown

126

Master 119
For use with TE pp. T434d–T434e

STUDENT WRITING SAMPLE

Read this story.
Think about how well it is written.
Give it a score. Circle the number.

Development of Ideas
Score
1   2   3   4

After the Hurricane

Drip, drip, drip. I could hear the raindrops as they fell from the roof. At least the roof is still there, I thought.

Seconds later, my dad opened the door to the closet. It was not a very big place. My whole family had been hiding there, ever since we heard that a hurricane was coming.

My mother, father, brother, and I climbed up from the floor of the closet. We were sore from sitting for so long and from being so scared and tense. Slowly, we all looked around. Our dog got out of the closet, too.

The house didn't look the same at all! There was nothing on the walls. The furniture was turned over and torn or broken. Everywhere, there was trash. Torn-up paper, and broken pieces of our stuff were lying all around. The doors and all the windows were gone. Broken glass was everywhere. Air blew through the house.

The entire floor was covered in about three inches of water. My brother and I held hands with our parents. The walls and the furniture and trash lying around were all wet, too. It was like we had a rainstorm inside the house!

When we went in the kitchen, we saw that all the cupboards were open. They were empty, too. What will we eat? I thought.

I was right to worry! We didn't find anything to eat for a day and a half!

Evaluate Writing Samples
© Hampton-Brown

127

Master 120
For use with TE pp. T368d–T368e

STUDENT WRITING SAMPLE

Read this story.
Think about how well it is written.
Give it a score. Circle the number.

Blizzard Conditions

My big brother Rico ran out to the car. The rest of us were waiting inside it. Rico had his new driver's license, and he was going to take all the kids for a ride.

"It's supposed to snow again today," he said.

Where we grew up, the weather was hot all the time. We swam a lot and went to the beach. Here in our new home, there is snow and ice all winter long.

Rico backed the car out of the driveway and headed into the country. The snow was piled high. There was a cold wind, but we didn't care.

Suddenly, the wind got stronger. Snow started blowing across the road and across our windshield.

Rico stopped the car. He couldn't see anymore! He put on emergency flashers. We were scared. All around us was snow. The car was dark inside. It was very scary! We waited in the car and hoped the storm would stop.

Finally, it slowed down, and we could see out again. A woman with a snow plow came by. She said, "So is this your first blizzard?"

"Yes," we all yelled. She laughed and said to check the whole weather report next time.

Evaluate Writing Samples
© Hampton-Brown

128

Master 121
For use with TE pp. T434d–T434e

STUDENT WRITING SAMPLE

Read this story.
Think about how well it is written.
Give it a score. Circle the number.

Development of Ideas
Score

| 1 | 2 | 3 | 4 |

The Flood

There was a big flood in my town. I saw my grandmother outside. A firefighter carried Grandmama through the water. I watched from the upstairs window.

The sirens were loud. I covered my ears. Then I stopped because I wanted to hear what the firefighter was shouting. The firefighter told us to wait in the house. He said they could come back in a boat.

My family and I waited. We saw Grandmama going away in a truck with a lot of other people.

Pretty soon, the firefighters came back to the house. My sister and I got into one boat. Our mother got into the other boat.

Later, I looked around at the people in the shelter. Everyone was wet, tired, and worried. It seemed like the whole town was there.

Finally, my family got to go back to our house. Everything was damaged. People had to clean the mud and stains off everything in their houses. Later, everything went back to normal, but I will never forget the flood.

Evaluate Writing Samples
© Hampton-Brown

129

Master 122
For use with TE pp. T368d–T368e

Read this personal narrative.
Think about how well it is written.
Give it a score. Circle the number.

Voice
Score

1   2   3   4

The Soccer Team

On Monday, I saw a big sign at school. The sign said: "Try out for the soccer team Friday at 3:00." The minute I saw that sign, I knew I had to do it. Soccer is my favorite sport! I play soccer all the time with my cousins. I never miss a game on TV. I dream of being a professional soccer player someday.

I asked my cousin Rafael to help me get ready for the tryout. Every day after school, we ran up and down the soccer field. We kicked the ball back and forth and practiced our headers. I thought I might get a dent in my head from passing so many balls!

On Friday at 3:00, I went to the soccer field. The coach was Mr. Posada. He was also our gym teacher. I liked him because he always told jokes and made us laugh.

Mr. Posada made us run drills. Then he put us on teams and asked us to play a game. He took a lot of notes in his notebook. After three hours, the tryout was over. Mr. Posada said he would post the names of the team members on Monday.

On Monday, I saw the sheet of paper on the wall. My heart pounded. I held my breath and went over to read the names. Would mine be there? I couldn't think. I just had to look. Halfway down the list, I saw my name. I was on the team! Wait until Rafael and my family heard the good news. I could hardly believe it myself.

Evaluate Writing Samples
© Hampton-Brown

130

Master 123
For use with TE pp. T312d–T312e

STUDENT WRITING SAMPLE

Read this personal narrative.
Think about how well it is written.
Give it a score. Circle the number.

Voice
Score

1   2   3   4

Learning English

English is a hard language to learn. I know because I am trying to learn English right now. There are so many new sounds and words to learn, and some words mean more than one thing! That's hard.

My teacher's name is Ms. Madduri. She has patience. On the first day of class, she gave each of us a dictionary. It had words in both Spanish and English. She said, "When you get stuck, check in the dictionary." I use my dictionary all the time.

We talk about many different things in class. Sometimes we talk about the weather or our families or our favorite books. Each week one of the students has to give a show-and-tell talk. Once a month we take a trip somewhere.

Ms. Madduri asks us questions to help us practice speaking. She says we should try to speak English every chance we get. "Practice makes perfect" is Ms. Madduri's motto. I believe it's a very good motto.

I practice speaking English with my friends Brian and Cathy. They are a big help because they help me with some of the tricky words. There are a lot of tricky words.

I will work hard at learning English. One day I will be able to speak English in a good way, thanks to Ms. Madduri and my friends.

Evaluate Writing Samples
© Hampton-Brown

131

Master 124
For use with TE pp. T254d–T254e

STUDENT WRITING SAMPLE

Read this personal narrative.
Think about how well it is written.
Give it a score. Circle the number.

Big News

One day my mother came home from work. She was excited. She told me she had some news. She had a new job. It was in another state. "We will move to a new house, and you will go to a new school," she said.

I was sad and excited at the same time. There were lots of things I was going to miss at my old school, like my friends and playing on the softball team. I would miss my math teacher, Ms. Hart.

Then my mother told me about my new school. She said it had a pool. I could ride my bike to school. I could join the math club. My mother said I would like the new school.

My mother said we would move at the end of the school year. That way I could finish fourth grade in my old school. It would be easier to start at a new school in September.

Everyone knew I was moving at the end of the year. They were nice to me. They said they would write to me. They might even come to visit me in the summer, too.

On the last day of school, my teacher and friends had a good-bye party for me. They had balloons and a cake. They gave me a book of photos and wrote "good luck." That was nice.

Evaluate Writing Samples
© Hampton-Brown

132

Master 125
For use with TE pp. T312d–T312e

Read this personal narrative.
Think about how well it is written.
Give it a score. Circle the number.

Voice
Score

1   2   3   4

The School Band

I play the clarinet. I have played the clarinet since I was seven years old. First, Ms. Price was my teacher. Now I have lessons with Mr. Johnson. I practice all the time. On the weekends I spend a lot of time practicing.

This year I am in fifth grade. In fifth grade, students can try out for the school band. Band members wear a blue uniform. They have to practice a lot and stay after school.

The band tryouts are next week. I have to play a song for Ms. Summers. She is the band director. If I play well and don't make any mistakes, then maybe Ms. Summers will ask me to join the band. I don't know yet what song I'm going to play.

Last year, my brother tried out for the band. He plays the trumpet. Ms. Summers liked my brother's playing. So now my brother is in the band.

The band gets to play in the holiday concerts at our school. The band also marches in the Memorial Day parade. That is in May. It would be nice to be in the band.

Evaluate Writing Samples
© Hampton-Brown

133

Master 126
For use with TE pp. T254d–T254e

Avenues

Family Newsletters

Grandparents and Great-Grandparents

In this unit, we will be recalling stories about our ancestors.

1. Tell a story about your child's grandparents or great-grandparents.

2. Have your child draw a picture of that ancestor on the back of this page.

3. Have your child take notes about the story. Remind your child to bring the page to class.

What We're Reading

"Grandma's Records"
In this story, a boy learns to love music from his grandmother.

"We Honor Our Ancestors"
Four artists share their family stories, traditions, and pride in their heritage through art and stories.

BOLETÍN Avenues

Abuelos y bisabuelos

En esta unidad, recordaremos a nuestros antepasados.

1. Comparta con su hijo o hija un cuento sobre un abuelo o bisabuelo.

2. Pida a su hijo o hija que, al otro lado de esta hoja, haga un dibujo de ese familiar.

3. Pida a su hijo o hija que tome apuntes sobre el cuento. Recuérdele que debe traer esta hoja a la clase.

Estamos leyendo...

"Los discos de mi abuela"
En este cuento, una abuela comparte su amor a la música con su nieto.

"En honor a nuestros antepasados"
Cuatro artistas transmiten su orgullo cultural y comparten historias y tradiciones familiares.

TIN THƯ Avenues

Ông Bà Và Ông Bà Cố

Trong tín chỉ này, chúng ta sẽ nhớ lại những câu chuyện về tổ tiên của chúng ta.

1. Kể một câu chuyện về ông bà và ông bà cố của con quý vị.

2. Bảo con của quý vị vẽ một tấm hình về vị tổ tiên này trên mặt sau của tờ giấy này.

3. Bảo con của quý vị ghi chú về câu chuyện. Nhắc em mang tờ giấy này vào lớp học.

Chúng Ta Đang Đọc Những Gì

"Hồ Sơ Của Bà"

Trong chuyện này, một cậu bé học cách yêu âm nhạc từ bà của cậu.

"Chúng Ta Vinh Danh Tổ Tiên Của Chúng Ta"

Bốn nhà nghệ sĩ kể cho nhau nghe những lịch sử và truyền thống của gia đình họ, và hãnh diện trong những di sản của họ qua nghệ thuật và những câu chuyện.

Avenues 教育通讯

祖父母和曾祖父母

在这一单元里，我们将重温我们祖先的故事。

1. 讲一个你孩子的祖父母或曾祖父母的故事。

2. 让你的孩子在这张纸的背面画出这位祖先的画像。

3. 让你的孩子记下故事的要点。提醒你的孩子上课时带上这张纸。

读书目录

《祖母的唱片》
在这个故事里,一个小男孩受他祖母的影响而酷爱音乐。

《尊崇我们的祖先》
四位艺术家通过他们的作品描写他们的家族史和家族遗产。

Avenues 뉴스레터

조부모와 증조부

이 유닛에서는 선조들에 대한 이야기를 나눌 것입니다.

1. 자녀의 조부모 또는 증조부에 대하여 자녀에게 얘기해 주세요.

2. 이 페이지 뒷면에 그 선조의 그림을 그리라고 하십시오.

3. 그 이야기에 대하여 적으라고 하십시오. 적은 것을 클래스에 갖고 가라고 하십시오.

우리가 읽고 있는 책들

"할머니의 음악 레코드"
한 소년이 할머니로부터 음악에 대한 사랑을 배운다.

"선조들을 존중"
4명의 화가들이 자신들의 가족 이야기, 전통, 그리고 자신들의 유산에 대한 긍지를 그림과 이야기로 나눈다.

Niampog-txivyawg-Niamtais-yawmtxiv thiab Pojkoob-Yawgkoob

Nyob rau tshoojntawv no, peb yuav rov tig mus kawm txog peb tej pojkoob-yawgkoob.

1. Qhia ib zaj lus txog koj tus menyuam cov niampog-txivyawg niamtais-yawmtxiv thiab pojkoob-yawgkoob.

2. Hais kom koj tus menyuam kos ib daim duab txog nej pojkoob-yawgkoob rau daim nplooj ntawv no sab nrauv.

3. Hais kom koj tus menyuam sau zaj lus tseg. Nco ntsoov hais kom koj tus menyuam nqa daim ntawv no tuaj tom nws chav tsev kawmntawv.

Tej Peb Nyeem Txog

"Tej Pog Khaws Tseg"

Nyob rau zaj lus no, tus menyuam tub paub nyiam kwvtxhiaj los yog vim los ntawm nws pog los.

"Peb Hawm Txog Peb Tej Pojkoob Yawg Koob"

Plaub tug neeg kos duab lawv kos duab qhia txog lawv tsev neeg lub keebkwm, lawv tej kev coj noj coj ua thiab tej kablig kev cai uas muaj nqi heev rau lawv.

BILTEN Avenues

Gran paran, Gran Gran Paran

Nan leson sa a, nou pral sonje istwa zansèt nou yo.

1. Rakonte yon istwa sou gran paran, ak gran gran paran pitit ou a.

2. Mande pitit ou a desinen yon imaj zansèt sa a sou do fèy sa a.

3. Mande pitit ou pran nòt sou istwa sa a. Fè li sonje pote fèy la nan klas la.

Kisa Nap Li

"Kaye Nòt Grann Yo"
Nan istwa sa a, yon ti gason aprann renmen mizik menm jan ak grann ni.

"Nap Onore Zansèt Nou Yo"
Kat atis ap pataje istwa, tradisyon ak fyète fanmi yo nan travay atistik yo ak nan istwa yo ekri.

_____

_____

_____

_____

_____

_____

_____

Avenues Newsletter

Why Is Grass Green?

In this unit, we will be learning about the Earth.

1. Share a story or myth with your child about how and why something on the Earth came to be.

2. Have your child draw a picture on the back of this page to remind him or her about the myth.

3. Have your child take notes about the story. Remind your child to bring the notes and picture to class.

What We're Reading

"Piecing Earth and Sky Together"
This Laotian myth tells how the Earth was made and teaches the values of hard work and patience.

"Planet Earth/Inside Out"
This science article explains how Earth changes.

BOLETÍN Avenues

¿Por qué es verde el pasto?

En esta unidad, aprenderemos sobre la Tierra.

1. Comparta con su hijo o hija un mito que explique la existencia de algo en la Tierra.

2. Pida a su hijo o hija que, al otro lado de esta hoja, haga un dibujo que le recuerde el mito.

3. Ayude a su hijo o hija a tomar apuntes. Recuérdele que debe traer esta hoja a la clase.

Estamos leyendo...

"Juntando cielo y Tierra"
Este mito laosiano explica cómo se formó la Tierra y muestra el valor de la diligencia y la paciencia.

"La Tierra por dentro y por fuera"
Este artículo de ciencias explica los cambios de la Tierra.

TIN THƯ Avenues

Tại Sao Cỏ Màu Xanh?

Trong tín chỉ này, chúng ta sẽ học về Trái Đất.

1. Kể cho con quý vị nghe một câu chuyện hay một huyền thoại nói về bằng cách nào và tại sao một vật có mặt trên Trái Đất.

2. Bảo con của quý vị vẽ một tấm hình trên mặt sau tờ giấy này để nhắc em nhớ về huyền thoại này.

3. Bảo con của quý vị ghi chú lại câu chuyện đó. Nhắc em mang lời ghi chú này và tấm hình vào lớp học.

Chúng Ta Đang Đọc Những Gì

"Đặt Trái Đất Và Bầu Trời Lại Với Nhau"

Huyền thoại của người Lào này kể về cách Trái Đất được tạo lập như thế nào và dạy về những giá trị của sự cần cù và nhẫn nại.

"Hành Tinh Trái Đất / Bề Trong Ra Ngoài"

Bài báo khoa học này giải thích Trái Đất thay đổi như thế nào.

Avenues 教育通讯

草为什么是绿色的？

我们将在这一单元里学习地球的知识。

1. 和你的孩子分享关于地球上的某事物流传至今的故事或神话。

2. 让你的孩子在这张纸的背面画出这一神话的大意。

3. 让你的孩子记下故事的要点。提醒孩子上课时带上写的笔记和画的画。

读书目录

《把地球和天空连接到一起》
这个老挝神话在描述地球是如何形成的同时，颂扬了勤劳和忍耐的美德。

《行星地球/从内到外》
这篇科技文章解释了地球是如何变化的。

Avenues 뉴스레터

풀은 왜 초록색인가?

이 유닛에서는 지구에 대하여 배웁니다.

1. 지구가 어떻게 만들어졌는지 이야기나 신화를 자녀에게 얘기해 주십시오.

2. 이 페이지 뒷면에 그 신화와 관련된 그림을 그리라고 하십시오.

3. 그 이야기에 대하여 적으라고 하십시오. 적은 것과 그림을 클래스에 갖고 가라고 하십시오.

우리가 읽고 있는 책들

"지구와 하늘을 함께 꽤어 뚫기"

이 라오스의 전설은 지구가 어떻게 만들어졌는지 설명하고 인내와 부지런함의 미덕을 가르친다.

"혹성 지구/속을 뒤집어 보기"

지구가 어떻게 변하는지 설명하는 과학 이야기.

Vim Li Cas Nyom Thiaj Li Ntsuab?

Nyob rau tshoojntawv no, peb yuav kawm txog lub ntiajteb av.

1. Piav rau koj tus menyuam mloog txog tej lus los sis tej dabneeg thaum ub uas qhia txog tias vim li cas thiaj li muaj thooj av.

2. Hais kom koj tus menyuam kos ib daim duab rau daim nplooj ntawv no sab nrauv kom pab nws nco tau txog zaj dabneeg.

3. Hais kom koj tus menyuam muab zaj lus sau tseg. Nco ntsoov hais kom koj tus menyuam nqa zaj lus thiab daim duab tuaj tom nws chav tsev kawmntawv.

Tej Peb Nyeem Txog

"Muab Lub Ntiajteb Av thiab Lub Ntuj Coj Los Sib Dhos"

Zaj dabneeg nplog no piav txog tias vim li cas thiaj muaj thooj av thiab qhia txog tias kam sivzog ua haujlwm thiab kam ua neeg siab ntev no muaj nqis npaum cas.

"Lub Ntiajteb Av Sab Hauv Ua Sab Nrauv"

Tsab ntawv science no piav txog tias lub ntiajteb av hloov li cas.

BILTEN Avenues

Poukisa Zèb Gen Koulè Vèt?

Nan leson sa a nou pral aprann konnen latè.

1. Rakonte pitit ou a yon istwa oubyen yon lejann ki eksplike kijan ak pou ki rezon yon bagay sou Latè te rive fèt.

2. Mande pitit ou a desinen yon imaj sou do fèy sa a pou li ka sonje lejann nan.

3. Mande pitit ou a pran nòt sou istwa sa a. Fè li sonje pote nòt li yo ak imaj la nan klas la.

Kisa Nap Li

"Ann Met Syèl ak Tè Ansanm"
Lejann sa a ki soti nan peyi "Laòs" rakonte kijan Latè te fèt epi li pale sou enpòtans travay di ak aprann pran pasyans.

"Latè Lanvè Landwat"
Atik syantifik sa a dekri kijan Latè a chanje.

Avenues NEWSLETTER

Family Dance

In this unit, we will be learning about how our bodies move.

1. Do you have a favorite dance? Teach your child some of the dance steps.

2. Have your child practice the steps so he or she can demonstrate the dance in class.

3. Have your child take notes about the dance and what it is called in your home language.

What We're Reading

"Dancing Wheels"

This photo essay introduces an amazing dance troupe that includes dancers in wheelchairs.

"Moving"

This science article explains how bones, joints, and muscles work together to keep a body moving.

BOLETÍN Avenues

Baile familiar

En esta unidad, aprenderemos cómo se mueve nuestro cuerpo.

1. ¿Hay algún baile que le guste? Enseñe algunos pasos a su hijo o hija.

2. Pida a su hijo o hija que practique el baile para demostrarlo en la clase.

3. Pida a su hijo o hija que apunte el nombre del baile y otros detalles.

Estamos leyendo...

"Ruedas que bailan"
Este ensayo fotográfico presenta una compañía de danza que incluye bailarines en sillas de ruedas.

"En movimiento"
Este artículo de ciencias explica cómo se mueve el cuerpo con la ayuda de los huesos, las coyunturas y los músculos.

TIN THƯ Avenues

Khiêu Vũ Gia Đình

Trong tín chỉ này, chúng ta sẽ học về cách cơ thể của chúng ta di chuyển như thế nào.

1. Quý vị có điệu khiêu vũ nào ưa thích không? Hãy dạy cho con của quý vị một vài bước nhảy trong điệu khiêu vũ này.

2. Bảo con của quý vị thực tập những bước nhảy đó sao cho em có thể trình diễn điệu khiêu vũ này trong lớp học.

3. Bảo con của quý vị ghi chú lại điệu khiêu vũ này và tên gọi của nó bằng tiếng mẹ đẻ của quý vị.

Chúng Ta Đang Đọc Những Gì

"Những Bánh Xe Nhảy Múa"
Bài luận ảnh này giới thiệu một đoàn khiêu vũ thượng thặng gồm có các vũ viên ngồi trên xe lăn.

"Di Chuyển"
Bài báo khoa học này giải thích cách các xương, khớp xương và bắp thịt cùng hoạt động như thế nào để giữ cho cơ thể tiếp tục di chuyển.

Avenues 教育通讯

家庭舞蹈

在这一单元里，我们将学习我们的身体是如何运动的。

1. 你是否特别喜欢跳某一种舞蹈？教你的孩子几个舞步。

2. 让你的孩子练习这些舞步以便可以在课堂上表演。

3. 让你的孩子记下有关这一舞蹈的要点以及它在你的母语中的名称。

读书目录

《车轮之舞》
这组照片介绍了一个令人惊叹的，有残疾人舞蹈家的舞蹈团。

《运动》
这篇科技文章解释了人体的骨头、关节和肌肉，他们如何互相配合来保持身体运动的。

패밀리 댄스

이 유닛에서는 우리 몸이 어떻게 움직이는지 배웁니다.

1. 한국 춤을 알고 있나요? 자녀에게 몇 가지 춤 스텝을 가르쳐 주세요.

2. 클래스 앞에서 보여줄 수 있도록 스텝을 연습하라고 하십시오.

3. 그 춤에 대하여 적고 한국어로 그 이름을 적으라고 하십시오.

우리가 읽고 있는 책들

"춤추는 휠"

이 사진 에세이는 휠체어 탄 춤꾼이 포함된 댄스 그룹을 소개한다.

"동작"

뼈와 관절, 그리고 근육이 어떻게 상호 작용하면서 몸을 움직이는지 설명.

Tsevneeg Tsaj Dhia Las-voos

Nyob rau tshoojntawv no, peb yuav kawm txog tias peb tej cev txav tau mus los li cas.

1. Puas muaj tej hom kev tsaj dhia las-voos uas koj nyiam tshaj plaws? Qhia koj tus menuam xyaum ua ruam las-voo.

2. Hais kom koj tus menyuam xyaum dhia es nws thiaj paub coj tuaj ua qhia rau nws chav tsev kawmntawv.

3. Hais kom koj tus menyuam muab zaj tsaj-dhia ntawd coj los sau tseg, tsis tag li ua li nej yam lus ne luag muab zaj tsaj-dhia ntawd tis npe li cas.

Tej Peb Nyeem Txog

"Cov Kauj Log Tsaj Dhia"
Daim duab thiab cov lus qhia kom peb paub txog pab tub ntxhais las voos uas muaj cov zaum hauv rooj thob-log nrog.

"Tsiv Chawv"
Tsab ntawv science no piav txog tias cov txha, cov qij txha thiab tej leeg ua haujlwm ua ke li cas es thiaj pab tau lub cev txav tau mus los.

BILTEN Avenues

Dans Fanmi

Nan leson sa a, nou pral aprann kijan kò nou mache.

1. Èske genyen yon dans ou pi pito? Aprann pitit ou a kèk pa nan dans sa a.

2. Mande pitit ou a pou li fè pa sa yo pou li sa montre rès klas la yo.

3. Mande pitit ou a pran kèk nòt sou dans la epi ekri li nan pwòp lang ni.

Kisa Nap Li

"Dansè nan Chèz Woulan"

Ansanm foto sa yo montre yon twoup dansè ekstraòdinè kap danse sou chèz woulan.

"Mouvman"

Atik syantifik sa a ap eksplike nou kouman zo, jwenti ak misk nou travay ansanm pou fè kò nou mache.

Our Own History

In this unit, we will be learning about important events in early American history.

1. Tell your child about important events in your home country's history.

2. Have your child take notes. Remind your child to bring the notes to class.

What We're Reading

"Joining the Boston Tea Party"
In this story, a brother and sister travel back in time to participate in an important event in American history.

"George Washington"
This biography tells about George Washington, the first president of the United States.

BOLETÍN Avenues

Nuestra historia

En esta unidad, aprenderemos sobre la época temprana de la historia americana.

1. Comenten juntos algunos sucesos importantes en la historia de su país de origen.

2. Ayude a su hijo o hija a tomar apuntes. Recuérdele que debe traer esta hoja a la clase.

Estamos leyendo…

"La fiesta del té de Boston"

En este cuento, unos hermanos viajan a través del tiempo para participar en un evento importante de la historia americana.

"George Washington"

Esta biografía habla de George Washington, el primer presidente de los Estados Unidos.

TIN THƯ Avenues

Lịch Sử Của Chúng Ta

Trong tín chỉ này, chúng ta sẽ học về những biến cố quan trọng trong giai đoạn đầu của lịch sử Hoa Kỳ.

1. Kể cho con của quý vị nghe về những biến cố quan trọng trong lịch sử đất nước quê hương của quý vị.

2. Bảo con của quý vị ghi chú lại. Nhắc em mang lời ghi chú này vào lớp học.

Chúng Ta Đang Đọc Những Gì

"Tham Dự Buổi Tiệc Trà Boston"

Trong chuyện này, một người anh và cô em gái thực hiện cuộc hành trình quay trở lại kịp thời dự một biến cố quan trọng trong lịch sử Hoa Kỳ.

"George Washington"

Bài tiểu sử này kể về George Washington, vị tổng thống đầu tiên của Hoa Kỳ.

Avenues 教育通讯

上溯我们的历史

在这一单元里，我们将学习早期美国历史中的重要事件。

1. 给孩子讲讲你的故国历史中的重要事件。

2. 让孩子记下要点，提醒你的孩子上课时带上写的笔记。

读书目录

《参加波士顿茶会》

在这个科幻故事中，一对兄妹逆时旅行去参与美国历史上的一次重要事件。

《乔治·华盛顿》

这一传记讲述了美国第一任总统乔治华盛顿 (George Washington) 的一生。

Avenues 뉴스레터

우리 자신의 역사

이 유닛에서는 미국 초기의 역사에서 중요한 사건들을 배웁니다.

1. 고국의 역사 중에 중요한 사건들을 자녀에게 얘기해 주세요.

2. 들은 것을 적으라고 하세요. 적은 것을 클래스에 갖고 가라고 하십시오.

우리가 읽고 있는 책들

"보스턴 티 파티"
한 오누이가 과거의 시간으로 여행하여 미국 역사의 중요한 사건에 참여한다.

"조지 워싱턴"
미국 초대 대통령 조지 워싱턴의 자서전.

Peb Tus Kheej Lub Keebkwm

Nyob rau tshoojntawv no, peb yuav kawm txog tej ub tej no yav tag los uas tseemceeb heev rau Asmeslivkas lub keebkwm.

1. Qhia rau koj tus menyuam txog tej yam uas tseemceeb heev nyob rau koj lub tebchaws lub keebkwm.

2. Hais kom koj tus menyuam muab sau tseg. Nco ntsoov hais kom koj tus menyuam nqa daim ntawv sau tuaj tom nws chav tsev kawmntawv.

Tej Peb Nyeem Txog

"Mus Koom Nrog Boston Tea Party"

Nyob rau zaj lus no, ob nus muag tau rov qab tig sijhawm mus koom raus tes ua ib txog haujlwm tseemceeb heev pab rau Asmeslivkas lub keebkwm.

"George Washington"

Zaj lus piav txog thawj tug thawjcoj nyob rau hauv United States lub neej – tus thawjcoj yog George Washington.

BILTEN Avenues

Pwòp Istwa Nou

Nan leson sa a, nou pral apran evènman enpòtan sou istwa Damerik.

1. Rakonte pitit ou a evènman enpòtan yo ki nan istwa peyi w.

2. Fè pitit ou a pran nòt sou sa. Fè li sonje pote nòt yon nan klas la.

Kisa Nap Li

"Ann Ale nan 'Boston Tea Party' an"

Nan istwa sa a, yon frè ak sè ap reviv nan tan lontan, evènman enpòtan nan istwa Damerik.

"Jòj Wachintonn"

Biyografi sa a rakonte istwa lavi Jòj Wachintonn, premye prezidan peyi Etazini.

Avenues NEWSLETTER

Fictional Characters

In this unit, we will read about places in the United States that were formed in impossible ways—by a family of giants!

1. Tell your child a tale that involves funny or larger-than-life characters.

2. Have your child make a comic strip about the tale, and share it with the class.

What We're Reading

"Greetings from America"
This travel article describes many beautiful places in the United States.

"The Bunyans"
This tall tale tells how a family of giants shaped the land of the United States.

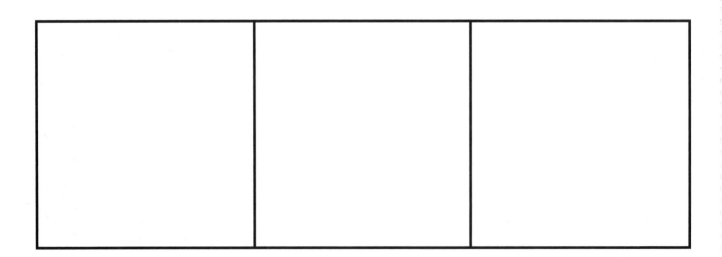

BOLETÍN Avenues

Personajes ficticios

En esta unidad, leeremos sobre lugares en los Estados Unidos que fueron formados de manera imposible: ¡por una familia de gigantes!

1. Cuéntele a su hijo o hija un cuento que contiene personajes exagerados.

2. Pida a su hijo o hija que haga una tira cómica. Puede usar la tira cómica para contar el cuento, para después compartirlo con la clase.

Estamos leyendo…

"Saludos desde Estados Unidos"
Este artículo turístico describe varios lugares bellos en los Estados Unidos.

"Los Bunyan"
Este cuento exagerado describe cómo una familia de gigantes formó el paisaje de los Estados Unidos.

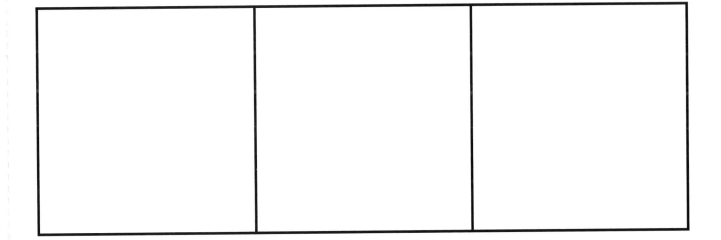

Những Nhân Vật Giả Tưởng

Trong tín chỉ này, chúng ta sẽ đọc về những nơi chốn tại Hoa Kỳ đã được thành lập một cách không thể thực hiện được—bởi một gia đình của người khổng lồ!

1. Kể cho con của quý vị nghe một chuyện cổ tích liên quan đến những nhân vật kỳ lạ hoặc to lớn hơn ngoài đời.

2. Trên mặt sau của trang giấy này, bảo con của quý vị vẽ trên những cái hộp giống như sau đây. Em có thể dùng những hộp này để tạo thành một dãy truyện bằng tranh về câu chuyện cổ tích đó, và mang vào lớp học cho mọi người xem.

Chúng Ta Đang Đọc Những Gì

"Lời Chào Từ Châu Mỹ"
Bài báo du hành này diễn tả nhiều nơi xinh đẹp tại Hoa Kỳ.

"Bunyans"
Chuyện cổ khó tin này kể về một gia đình của những người khổng lồ tạo dựng hình dáng đất đai tại Hoa Kỳ.

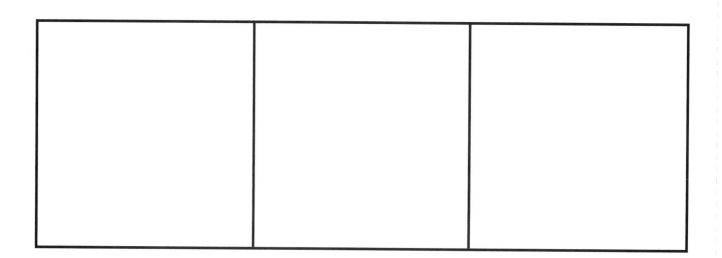

Avenues 教育通讯

传说中的人物

我们将在这个单元里读到由巨人家族造就的、难以想象而巧夺天工的胜地。

1. 告诉你的孩子一个其中有滑稽角色或巨型角色的传说。

2. 在这张纸的背面让你的孩子画出与下面相似的方框。他或她可以用这些方框画出一组描述这个传说的漫画，并和同学们分享。

读书目录

《来自美国的问候》
这篇旅游文章介绍了美国许多的旅游胜地。

《班扬一家》
这个民间故事讲述了一个巨人家族造就美国大地的故事。

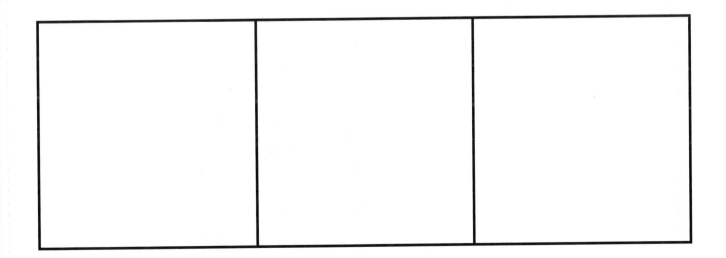

Newsletter 5 in Chinese

Avenues 뉴스레터

동화 속의 인물

이 유닛에서는 한 거인 가족이 주물러 만들었다는 미국의 땅에 대하여 배웁니다.

1. 우습거나 과장된 인물이 등장하는 동화를 자녀에게 말해주세요.

2. 페이지 뒷면에 아래와 같은 박스를 그리라고 하십시오. 자녀는 박스를 이용하여 동화를 만화 형식으로 그려 클래스에 갖고 가라고 하십시오.

우리가 읽고 있는 책들

"미국이 인사 드립니다"
미국의 많은 아름다운 장소를 소개.

"버니언스"
한 거인 가족이 미국의 땅을 주물러 만들었다는 전래 동화.

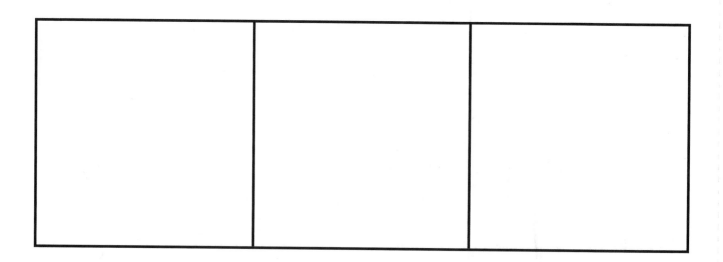

Cov Yeebyam Khwv Yees

Nyob rau tshoojntawv no, peb yuav nyeem txog tej chaw nyob rau United States uas zoo txawv txawv – vim tsevneeg nyav yog cov ua!

1. Qhia rau koj tus menyuam txog tej zaj dabneeg uas hais txog tej yam dab tsi txaus luag los sis tej yam uas loj tshaj qhov nws loj tau.

2. Nyob daim nplooj ntawv no sab nrauv, hais kom koj tus menyuam kos ib co kem zoo li cov no, es kos duab ua yeebyam txog zaj dabneeg rau, thiab coj tuaj piav rau chav tsev kawmntawv.

Tej Peb Nyeem Txog

"Asmeslivkas Xa Xov Nug Moo thiab Foom Koob Hmoo"

Tsab ntawv mus kev no piav txog tej chaw zoo zoo nkauj nyob rau tebchaws United States.

"The Bunyans"

Zaj dabneeg no qhia txog tias tsevneeg nyav loj loj lawv ua li cas es lawv thiaj li hloov tau thooj av nyob rau United States.

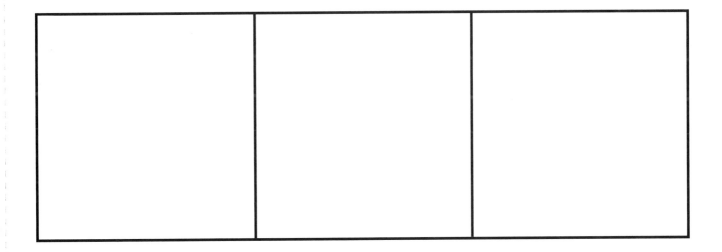

BILTEN Avenues

Karaktè Imajinè

Nan leson sa a, nou pral li sou tout jèfò yon fanmi jeyan te fè pou li devlope de kote nan peyi Etazini lè bagay yo te trè difisil!

1. Rakonte pitit ou a yon istwa sou yon moun ki komik anpil oubyen sou karaktè ki gen anpil enpòtans.

2. Mande pitit ou fè plizyè kare nan do fèy sa a tankou sa yo. Li ka sèvi ak kare sa yo pou li desinen ti komik ki va dekri istwa sa a, epi li va montre lòt elèv yo nan klas la.

Kisa Nap Li

"Etazini voye di Bonjou"
Atik sa a sou vwayaj dekri anpil bèl kote nan peyi Etazini.

"Bunyans-yo"
Kont sa a rakonte kijan yon fanmi jeyan te devlope peyi Etazini.

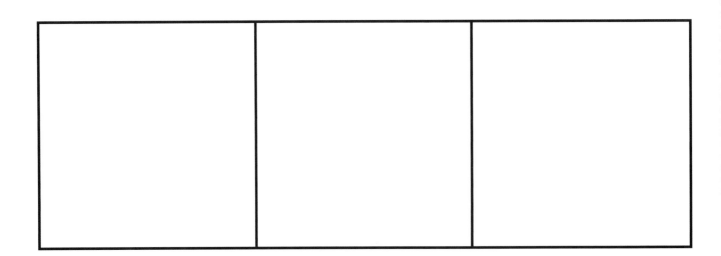

Proverbs from Home

In this unit, we will be learning about Ben Franklin and his experiments with electricity. Ben Franklin is also known for his wise sayings.

1. Share a proverb or saying from your home culture that you learned as a child. Explain the meaning of the proverb.

2. Have your child write down the proverb in your home language and in English. Remind your child to bring the notes to class to share the proverb with classmates.

What We're Reading

"Ben Franklin's Experiment"
This play introduces readers to the American inventor Ben Franklin and his experiments with electricity.

"Switch On, Switch Off"
This science article explains how electricity works.

BOLETÍN Avenues

¡Electrifica!

Dichos y refranes

En esta unidad, aprenderemos sobre Ben Franklin y sus experimentos con la electricidad.

Ben Franklin también es famoso por sus dichos y refranes.

1. Comparta un dicho o refrán que usted aprendió en su niñez. Explique el significado del dicho o refrán.

2. Pida a su hijo o hija que anote el dicho en español y en inglés. Recuérdele que debe traer esta hoja a la clase para compartir con sus compañeros.

Estamos leyendo...

"El experimento de Ben Franklin"
Esta obra de teatro presenta al inventor Ben Franklin y sus experimentos con la electricidad.

"Prende y apaga"
Este artículo de ciencias explica cómo funciona la electricidad.

172

Newsletter 6 in Spanish

TIN THƯ Avenues

Nhựng Câu Tục Ngữ Từ Quê Nhà

Trong tín chỉ này, chúng ta sẽ học về Ben Franklin và những thí nghiệm của ông ta với dòng điện. Ben Franklin cũng nổi tiếng về những câu nói khôn ngoan của ông.

1. Nói cho con của quý vị biết một câu tục ngữ hay lời nói từ nền văn hoá quê nhà của quý vị mà quý vị đã học được khi còn bé. Giải thích ý nghĩa của câu tục ngữ này.

2. Bảo con của quý vị viết câu tục ngữ đó bằng thứ tiếng nói của quý vị và bằng tiếng Anh. Nhắc con của quý vị mang lời ghi chú này vào lớp học để chia xẻ câu tục ngữ này với các bạn cùng lớp.

Chúng Ta Đang Đọc Những Gì

"Thí Nghiệm Của Ben Franklin"

Vở kịch này giới thiệu cho người đọc về nhà phát minh Ben Franklin và những cuộc thí nghiệm của ông ta với dòng điện.

"Bật Mở, Bật Tắt"

Bài báo khoa học này giải thích điện lực hoạt động ra sao.

_____

_____

_____

_____

_____

_____

_____

Avenues 教育通讯

家庭谚语

在这一单元里我们将学习本·富兰克林 (Ben Franklin) 和他的发电实验。本·富兰克林还有妙语连珠的名声。

1. 讲述一个你孩提时学会的故乡的谚语或传说并解释这一谚语的含义。

2. 让孩子分别用你的母语和英语写下这一谚语。提醒你的孩子上课时带上写的笔记，和同学们分享这一谚语。

读书目录

《本·富克林的实验》
这个剧本向读者介绍了美国发明家本·富兰克林 (Ben Franklin) 和他各种电的实验。

《拉闸，合闸》
这篇科技文章解释了电的工作原理。

한국의 속담

이 유닛에서는 벤 프랭클린과 그의 전기 실험에 대하여 배웁니다. 벤 프랭클린은 또한 잠언으로도 유명합니다.

1. 여러분이 어릴 때 한국에서 들은 속담이나 잠언을 자녀에게 얘기해 주세요. 속담의 의미를 설명해 주세요.

2. 한글과 영어로 속담을 적어보라고 하십시오.

우리가 읽고 있는 책들

"벤 프랭클린의 실험"
미국의 발명가 벤 프랭클린과 그의 전기 실험을 소개한다.

"스위치를 껐다 껐다"
전기의 작동 원리를 설명한다.

Zaj Pajlug Xa Tom Tsev Tuaj

Nyob rau tshoojntawv no, peb yuav kawm txog Ben Franklin thiab txog nws cov hluav taws xob uas nws khwv tswvyim ua. Neeg kuj paub Ben Franklin vim nws kuj txawj tham heev.

1. Qhia ib zaj pajlug los yog ib zaj lus uas nej haiv neeg nyiam muab hais ua kev pivtxwv pub rau koj tus menyuam mloog. Txhais rau nws tias zaj pajlug ntawd yog hais txog dab tsi.

2. Hais kom koj tus menyuam muab zaj pajlug sau ua nej hom lus thiab sau ua lus Askiv. Nco ntsoov hais kom koj tus menyuam nqa zaj lus thiab daim duab coj tuaj piav qhia rau nws chav tsev kawmntawv mloog.

Tej Peb Nyeem Txog

"Qhov Ben Franklin Tau Sim Ua"

Zaj yeebyam no qhia rau cov neeg nyeem ntawv kom lawv paub txog tus neeg Asmeslivkas uas nyiam khwv tswvyim ua ub ua no uas muaj lub npe hu ua Ben Franklin thiab txog nws cov hluav taws xob uas nws khwv tswvyim ua.

"Taws Kom Cig, Tua Kom Tuag"

Nyob rau tsab ntawv science no mas nws piav txog tias hluav taws xob ua haujlwm li cas.

Pwovèb Lakay

Nan leson sa a, nou pral aprann eksperyans Benn Franklenn te fè ak elektrisite. Benn Franklenn se yon nonm ke yo te rekonnèt trè byen pou bon pawòl li yo.

1. Pataje yon pwovèb oubyen yon pawòl nan kilti lakay ou ke ou te aprann lè ou te timoun. Eksplike sa pwovèb la vle di.

2. Fè pitit ou ekri pwovèb la nan pwòp lang ou ak nan lang anglè. Fè pitit ou an sonje pou li pote nòt yo nan klas la pou li montre lòt ti kanmarad li yo.

Kisa Nap Li

"Eksperyans Benn Franklenn yo"
Pyès teyat sa a entwodi enventè Ameriken yo te rele Benn Franklenn avèk eksperyans li te fè ak elektrisite.

"Limen, Etenn"
Atik syantifik sa a eksplike nou kouman elektrisite mache.

Avenues NEWSLETTER

Everyone Has a Story

In this unit, we will read about a time in U.S. history when the laws discriminated against African Americans. Author Pat McKissack tells, through a story and her autobiography, how people changed that.

1. Ask your child to tell you a story about a hard time in his or her life and how he or she overcame the problem.

2. Talk about what makes a good story.

3. Have your child take notes and bring the notes to class to use for a writing project later.

What We're Reading

"Goin' Someplace Special"
In this story, a young girl learns to believe in herself.

"Getting to Someplace Special"
Author Patricia McKissack explains how she and her husband make a good writing team.

_____

_____

_____

_____

_____

_____

_____

BOLETÍN Avenues

La historia de cada quien

En esta unidad, leeremos sobre un tiempo en la historia de los Estados Unidos en que las leyes discriminaban a los afro-americanos. La autora Patricia McKissack explica, con una historia y su autobiografía, cómo cambió esto.

1. Pida a su hijo o hija que le cuente cómo logró él o ella vencer un problema en su vida.

2. Comenten las cualidades de un buen cuento.

3. Pida a su hijo o hija que tome notas, y que las traiga a la clase para un proyecto de escritura más adelante.

Estamos leyendo…

"Un lugar especial"
En este cuento, una joven aprende a valorarse.

"Cómo llegar al lugar especial"
La autora Patricia McKissack explica cómo escriben juntos ella y su marido.

Mọi Người Đều Có Một Câu Chuyện

Trong tín chỉ này, chúng ta sẽ đọc về một thời kỳ trong lịch sử Hoa Kỳ khi luật pháp kỳ thị người Mỹ gốc Phi. Tác giả Pat McKissack kể, qua một câu chuyện và qua bài tự thuật về tiểu sử của mình, cách người dân đã thay đổi luật này như thế nào.

1. Yêu cầu con của quý vị kể cho quý vị nghe một câu chuyện về lúc khó khăn trong cuộc sống của em và cách em vượt qua khó khăn này.

2. Nói về những gì tạo thành một câu chuyện hay.

3. Bảo con của quý vị ghi chú và mang lời chi ghú này vào lớp học để sử dụng cho bài tập làm văn sau này.

Chúng Ta Đang Đọc Những Gì

"Đi Đến Một Nơi Đặc Biệt"

Trong chuyện này, một cô gái trẻ học được cách tự tin vào chính mình.

"Đến Được Một Nơi Đặc Biệt"

Tác giả Patricia McKissack giải thích cách bà ta và chồng đã cùng nhau viết văn tốt đẹp ra sao.

_____

_____

_____

_____

_____

_____

_____

_____

Avenues 教育通讯

人人都有故事讲

在这一单元里，我们将阅读有关那段在法律上歧视黑人的美国历史。作家帕特·麦可卡萨可通过一段故事和自传，讲述了人们是如何改变这种歧视的。

1. 让你的孩子讲自己遇到困难时和如何克服困难的故事。

2. 讨论一下是什么使一篇好故事获得成功。

3. 让你的孩子记下要点并且带到课堂上以便在今后的作文中使用。

读书目录

《去一个不同寻常的地方》
在这个故事里，一个小姑娘懂得了什么叫自信。

《到达不平凡的地方》
作家帕特丽夏·麦可卡萨可 (Patricia McKissack) 讲述了她和丈夫如何成了一支优秀的夫妻写作班。

누구든지 이야기를 갖고 있다

이 유닛에서는 흑인들을 법적으로 차별했던 미국 역사의 한 시대에 대하여 배웁니다. 작가 팻 맥기삭은, 이야기와 자신의 자서전을 통하여 사람들이 그러한 법을 어떻게 바꾸게 되었는지 이야기 합니다.

1. 차별대우로 어려움을 경험한적이 있었는지 그리고 어떻게 극복했는지 자녀에게 물어보십시오.

2. 어떤 이야기가 흥미있는지 말해 보십시오.

3. 글로 써서 나중에 작문 프로젝트에 사용하기 위해 클래스에 갖고 가라고 하십시오.

우리가 읽고 있는 책들

"특별한 곳에 가기"
한 소녀가 자신감을 키우는 과정.

"특별한 곳에 도착하기"
작가 패트리셔 맥기삭은 자신과 남편이 어떻게 팀이 되어 책을 쓰는가를 설명한다.

Txhua Leej Txhua Tus Yeej Muaj Lus Piav

Nyob rau tshoojntawv no, peb yuav nyeem txog U.S. lub keebkwm uas thaum ub lawv muaj txoj cai txiav cais tsis nyiam cov neeg dub African Americans. Tus kws sau ntawv Pat McKissack qhia tej no nyob rau hauv nws zaj lus thiab nyob rau hauv cov lus hais txog nws lub neej, tias neeg muab tej no hloov li cas.

1. Hais kom koj tus menyuam qhia txog ib qho kev txom nyem uas nws tau ntsib thiab kom nws qhia saib nws ua li cas es nws thiaj peem dhau tej teebmeem ntawd.

2. Tham txog tias dab tsi ua rau kom zaj lus zoo.

3. Hais kom koj tus menyuam muab sau tseg es nqa zaj lus tuaj tom nws chav tsev

Tej Peb Nyeem Txog

"Mus Rau Ib Qho Chaw Zoo Zoo"

Nyob rau zaj lus no, tus menyuam ntxhais kawm paub txog tias nws yuav tsum ntseeg nws tus kheej.

"Mus Txog Rau Ib Qho Chaw Zoo Zoo"

Tus neeg sau ntawv Patricia McKissck piav txog tej nws thiab nws tus txiv nkawd koomtes sib pab es nkawd thiaj sau tau ntawv zoo.

BILTEN Avenues

Chak Moun Gen Yon Istwa

Nan leson sa a, nou pral li yon istwa sou yon period nan Etazini lè lalwa lajistis tefè diskriminasyon kont moun nwa - afriken ameriken. Nan yon istwa ak nan otobiyografi li, ekriven Pat McKissack eksplike kijan pèp la resi rive chanje bagay sa yo.

1. Mande pitit ou a rakonte ou yon istwa sou yon lè li te genyen yon pwoblèm, epi kijan li te soti ladann.

2. Eksplike ki sa ki fè yon istwa vin enteresan.

3. Mande pitit ou a pran nòt epi pote yo nan klas la pou li sa aprann fè redaksyon.

Kisa Nap Li

"Nou Pral Yon Kote Espesyal"

Nan istwa sa a, yon jenn tifi aprann ganyen konfyans nan pwòp tèt li.

"Nou Pral Rive Yon Kote Espesyal"

Ekriven Patricia McKissack eksplike kijan li menm ak mari li fòme yon ekip solid lè yap ekri liv.

New Home, New Life

In this unit, we will be reading about why, when, and how people have come to the United States.

1. People have different reasons for moving to a new country. Help your child interview family members or friends who have immigrated to the United States.

2. Have your child list each person's name, his or her country of origin, and the reasons for moving to the United States. Remind your child to bring the list to class.

What We're Reading

"Calling the Doves"
In this story, the author tells about his family, California farmworkers who follow the harvest from field to field.

"Coming to America"
This social studies article explains how and when immigrants came to the United States.

BOLETÍN Avenues

Hogar nuevo, vida nueva

En esta unidad, aprenderemos por qué, cuándo y cómo han llegado inmigrantes a los Estados Unidos.

1. Existen varios motivos para emigrar a un nuevo país. Ayude a su hijo o hija a entrevistar a familiares o amigos que han llegado a los Estados Unidos.

2. Pida a su hijo o hija que anote el nombre de la persona, su país de origen y los motivos para venir a los Estados Unidos. Recuérdele que debe traer la lista a la clase.

Estamos leyendo...

"El canto de las palomas"

En este cuento, el autor habla de su familia, campesinos en California que siguen la cosecha de campo a campo.

"Vamos a los Estados Unido"

Este artículo de ciencias sociales describe la llegada de varios grupos de inmigrantes a los Estados Unidos.

Quê Hương Mới, Cuộc Sống Mới

Trong tín chỉ này, chúng ta sẽ đọc về lý do tại sao, khi nào và cách người ta đã và đang đến Hoa Kỳ.

1. Người ta có nhiều lý do khác nhau để di chuyển đến một quốc gia mới. Giúp con của quý vị phỏng vấn những thân nhân trong gia đình hay bạn bè đã di dân đến Hoa Kỳ

2. Bảo con của quý vị liệt kê tên từng người, tên quốc gia nguyên quán của người đó, và những lý do khiến họ di chuyển đến Hoa Kỳ. Nhắc em mang danh sách này vào lớp học.

Chúng Ta Đang Đọc Những Gì

"Gọi Những Con Chim Bồ Câu"

Trong chuyện này, tác giả kể về gia đình của ông, những nông dân ở California di chuyển theo mùa gặt từ cánh đồng này sang cánh đồng khác.

"Đến Mỹ Châu"

Bài báo nghiên cứu xã hội này giải thích những phương cách và thời điểm những di dân đến Hoa Kỳ.

新的家、新生活

在这一单元里，我们将读有关人们移民到美国的年代和历史原因。

1. 人们为了不同的原因才移民到陌生的国度。帮助你的孩子采访亲友们移民到美国来的动机。

2. 让你的孩子列出每个人的名字，来自何方以及移民到美国的原因。提醒你的孩子上课时带上记录。

读书目录

《召唤鸽子》
作者在这里讲述了他的一家 — 加利福尼亚州农工，在收获季节四处打工的故事。

《美国之梦》
这篇社会调查文章报告了美国的移民史。

Avenues 뉴스레터

낯설은 땅, 새로운 인생

이 유닛에서는 왜, 언제 , 그리고 어떻게 사람들이 미국에 왔는지 배웁니다.

1. 사람들은 각기 다른 이유로 미국으로 이민옵니다.미국으로 이민온 가족이나 친구를 인터뷰하도록 자녀를 도와주세요.

2. 인터뷰 한 각 사람의 이름과 고향 그리고 미국으로 이민 온 이유를 적으라고 하십시오.적은 명단을 클래스에 갖고 가라고 하십시오.

우리가 읽고 있는 책들

"콜링 더 더브즈"
작물을 따라 이동하는 멕시코에서 캘리포니아로 온 농장 노동자 가족의 이야기.

"커밍 투 아메리카"
사람들이 어떻게 그리고 언제 미국으로 이민오기 시작했는지 다루는 소셜 스터디.

Vajtsev Tshiab, Lub Neej Tshiab

Nyob rau tshoojntawv no, peb yuav nyeem txog tias vim li cas neeg thiaj tsiv tuaj nyob rau United States, tuaj thaum twg, thiab tuaj li cas.

1. Neeg nyias muaj nyias tswvyim ua rau nyias tsiv mus nyob rau lub tebchaws tshiab. Pab koj tus menyuam xam-phaj nws tsevneeg los sis cov phoojywg uas tsiv tuaj nyob rau United States.

2. Kom tus menyuam sau lawv cov npe, lub tebchaws lawv yug, thiab tej tswvyim ua rau lawv tsiv tuaj nyob United States. Hais kom tus menyuam nqa cov lus tuaj tom chav tsev kawmntawv.

Tej Peb Nyeem Txog

"Hu Cov Nquab"

Nyob rau zaj lus no, tus kws sau ntawv qhia txog nws tsevneeg, uas yog ib tsevneeg ua teb ntiav zog nyob rau California, lawv tsiv ib thaj teb mus rau ib thaj nyob ntawm saib thaj teb twg muaj sau qoob ntiav zog.

"Tuaj Rau Tebchaws Asmeslivkas"

Tsab ntawv txujci txog kev haumxeeb no piav txog tias cov neeg tsiv teb tsaws chaw lawv tsiv tuaj rau tebchaws United States no thaum twg, tuaj li cas rau li cas.

Kay Nèf, Lavi Nèf

Nan leson sa a, nou pral aprann kijan, kilè ak poukisa moun te vini Ozetazini.

1. Chak moun gen rezon pa li ki fè li deplase al viv nan yon lòt peyi. Ede pitit ou a fè yon entèvyou pou yon moun nan fanmi ni oubyen yon zanmi ki kite peyi li pou vin viv Ozetazini.

2. Mande pitit ou a pou li make non chak moun, ak peyi kote li soti, ak rezon ki fè li te vini Ozetazini. Fè pitit ou a sonje pou li pote lis non sa a nan klas la.

Kisa Nap Li

"Rele Zwezo Blan yo (colonmb)"
Nan ti istwa sa a, otè a pale de fanmi ni ki te kiltivatè nan leta Kalifòni epi ki tap fè rekòlt de yon tè a yon lòt.

"Vini nan Lamerik"
Atik syans sosyal sa a eksplike kijan ak kilè imigran yo te vini Ozetazini.
